QUEENS OF THE MAHABHARATA

KAVITA A. SHARMA

SECOND AND REVISED EDITION

© 2022, Kavita A. Sharma

Second and Revised Edition

All rights reserved.

No part of this publication may be reproduced, stored in a retrieval system, or transmitted, in any form or by any means, electronic, mechanical, photocopying, recording or otherwise, without the prior permission of the author. The author asserts the moral right to be identified as the author of this work

Cover photo BY NASA ON UNISPLASH

Cover design: Aryan Nath

Self-published by Dr. Kavita A. Sharma

PREFACE TO THE FIRST EDITION AND ACKNOWLEDGMENTS

The *Mahabharata* is a perennially fascinating and integral part of the Indian psyche. It is a truly pan-Indian text as wherever one goes throughout the length and breadth of the country, one hears stories of the Pandavas during their sojourn in the forests for thirteen years. The characters of the *Mahabharata* are as alive as if they are our contemporaries. We talk about them, praise, deride, dispute, and discuss them while we also venerate them. Every facet and nuance of life, every thought and feeling can be found in the *Mahabharata* in all its shades.

At first the *Mahabharata* seemed to be a completely male dominated text but as I gradually read it, I realized that the pivotal role is played more by the women than the men. While societal and familial structures subordinate them to the men, these brilliant and beautiful women subvert all the norms imposed on them to emerge as focal points of power and authority against all odds. Decisive and determined, they are the driving force of action egging the man to act. Once I realized this, my perspective changed radically. *The Queens of Mahabharata* is an effort to share some of my excitement of this discovery and to possibly enthuse the lay readers to have a look at the mirror-of-life text of the *Mahabharata*. It is a salute to the "never say die" spirit of women and their endurance in the face of all odds which is quite evident to anyone who cares to see. The trouble is that even today, so few do.

In this endeavour I would like to thank Delhi University for its change of syllabus a few years ago that set me probably on a lifelong journey of exploration of the different facets of the *Mahabharata*, which is truly inexhaustible. I have received support in my efforts from various institutions and organizations who have given me the opportunity to share my perceptions with them—some Delhi University Colleges and its Women's Studies and Development Centre, Banaras Hindu University, and the Indian Institute of Advanced Studies, to name only a few. My gratitude to Prof. Kapil Kapoor who always lent a willing and responsive ear to my perceptions of the *Mahabharata* whenever I chose to discuss them with him. To my dear friend Dr. Alka Raghuvanshi who shook me out of my inertia and saw to it that I write rather than just talk, I am grateful. Further, I can never thank my students enough who encouraged me by their keen interest and inquisitive questions forcing me to think and articulate. Last but not the least, I'd like to thank, Shri T.C. Arora who was ever willing to help and Smt. Rajesh Sharma for her untiring secretarial assistance. Without them, it would never have been possible to write.

Kavita A. Sharma

PREFACE TO THE SECOND AND REVISED EDITION

Queens of the Mahabharata was published by Rupa Publications in 2006, for which I am grateful. However, it went out of print and so it stayed on hold till I finished my formal professional assignments towards the end of 2019. It would have stayed this way had I realized that very diverse people remembered the book and asked about it. Schoolchildren, especially girls in senior classes, doing their projects on women's empowerment often turned to the powerful women characters of the *Mahabharata* and would get in touch with me. Several organizations would ask me to speak on the *Mahabharata* through the eyes of women including, much to my surprise, an organization of retired senior armed force officers had the same request. A condensed version was published as an article in an academic book. An academic-turned financial analyst and wealth manager from Canada happened to read the book and asked me to speak to a group of entrepreneurs and bankers, whom he was leading on a business trip to India. And thus, it went on. Finally, what was a game-changing acknowledgement of interest in the book came when Prof. Rita Paliwal, the head of the publishing Sasta Sahitya Mandal, the iconic publishing house established by Shri Jamnalal Vajaj and Shri G.D. Birla in 1925, inspired by the vision of Mahatma Gandhi, asked me to translate into Hindi, *The Queens of Mahabharata*. I undertook the task with some trepidation but eventually the outcome was good as, *Mahabharat ki Maharaniyaan*.

As I re-read the book in the process of translating it, I realized my ideas had grown and hence some revision was required. Also, the language needed tightening up and editing. Ms. Indu Ramchandani, a dear friend and an ace editor who can be relied upon to raise the script's level by her sheer editing skills, undertook to edit the book for me. For this I owe her a debt of gratitude.

Kavita A. Sharma

INTRODUCTION

Most of us have a peripheral awareness of the *Mahabharata*, assimilated from the stories that we have heard from our grandmothers or gleaned from the television serial that brought the country to a halt with its riveting power. But if we embark upon the adventure of reading the largest book in the world, which makes the claim that anything that is not in *Mahabharata* cannot be found anywhere else, we come across a fascinating array of characters, situations, and motivations that mirror our innermost desires and thoughts, which inevitably propel us into action. The text is an inalienable part of the Indian psyche, whose characters are so alive that they form an integral part of any politics, whether domestic or electoral.

This epic took about a thousand years to grow, as is generally believed, from *Jaya* to *Bharata* to *Mahabharata*. It not only exists in two major versions, the Northern and the Southern, but every region of India has contributed its own customs, myths, legends, folk tales, heroes, and heroines to it. Every subsequent generation has interpreted and reinterpreted the epic in its own way, to find justifications and solutions to the situations, conflicts and challenges that life may have thrown at it.

The *Mahabharata* showcases all "the shades of grey" of human nature and the immense difficulty of making ethical distinctions. This accounts for the excitement and perennial appeal attached to it. Unlike in the *Ramayana,* there are no ideal fathers, sons, mothers, and wives to be found in the *Mahabharata.* All unabashedly pursue their self-interest, the goal being power, wealth, and fulfilment of all desires. To the extreme extent, even Sri Krishna of the *Mahabharata,* who gives the Eternal Message of the Bhagavad Gita, which is intricately woven into the text of this epic, has 'shades' attributed to his very enigmatic persona. The tragedy of all the characters is as ours, stemming from narrow self-interest, which is finally self-defeating. That is why Sage Vyasa throws up his hands at the end of the Great War and cries out in anguish that wealth can be attained, and desires fulfilled only through dharma or righteousness, but no one ever listens, and no one ever will. How short-lived is human memory, is evident when Arjuna's great-grandson, Janamejaya, prepares for a great *yagna* to sacrifice the entire race of nagas to avenge the death of his father Parikshit, who dies of a snakebite by Takshaka, the king of the nagas. It takes only two generations to forget the horrors of the Great War and to begin the cycle of vengeance and destruction yet again.

But Sage Vyasa's desperate cry from the forest cannot go in vain. When a person as wise as this great sage talks of victory it cannot be merely physical victory; nor is it only the destruction of ignorance or the victory of dharma over adharma because that in any case must ultimately happen. What the great narrative conveys is a far deeper and significant message that such darkness will recur in time and that it will continue to cause an ambivalence and temporary corrosion in values. A person or history can only recount the occurrences, whether someone listens to them or not. Reading this narrative is an act of stepping back to witness the flow of the river of Time.

At the first obvious instance, the *Mahabharata* seems to be a story of men fighting a fratricidal war for the throne of Hastinapura, with its surrounding patriarchy that places no value on women, save for as wives and mothers of sons. But the more we read the text the more we acknowledge the courage of women such as Kunti, Satyavati, Gandhari, and Draupadi together with others who play minor roles. With the odds stacked against them, they use their minds and bodies to fight their own wars with a decisive and never-say-die attitude. They carve out pivotal places for themselves and play roles of such significance that the men have no option but to follow their lead. Where they cannot get their way directly, they subvert and manipulate but their fight is as much for the throne of Hastinapura as it is for their men. Yet, they are not petty. They are painted in heroic proportion, and we cannot help but be sympathetic, awe-struck, and stunned by their wisdom, cunning, craft and intellect, their immense enthusiasm to not only get the most that life has to offer but also to get it on their own terms.

So, is the justification of expediency and dissembling of true intent to gain power and wealth the message of the *Mahabharata*? Or does the *Mahabharata* bring all to grief, both the victorious and the defeated, as the victories are hollow, and often worse than the defeats. Is it an unrelenting picture of horrifying destruction and a lament over the futility of war?

Neither of these points of view can capture the centrality of this *mahakavya* or verse epic. It is a message of life that transcends death; a song of peace salvaged from the carnage of war; and finally, a sign of hope culled out from the spiritual desolation marking the end of the *Dvapara yuga*. It opens the path to transcending personal concerns and seeing that individual happiness can only be a part of everyone's happiness. It brings the message of the truly unconquerable state of mind that can accept with equanimity, happiness and unhappiness, likes and dislikes, whatever may come our way. It asks us to never accept defeat in our heart and to remain calm and hopeful even in moments of trial and great suffering. That is possibly why, the narrative begins with the lament of King Dhritarashtra, over-powered by his attachments and incapacities, and ends not only with a great sadness but also with the immense calm and peace that comes with a ripening and maturing obtained through sorrow and endurance.

1

THE QUEENS OF THE MAHABHARATA

The *Mahabharata* can be understood as a story of powerful women, asserting themselves in a patriarchal society. They are intelligent, accomplished, learned, well-versed in statecraft, beautiful and, when required, subversive. Unlike the average women, do not flounder at crucial moments but remain firm in their resolve. The most assertive of the women are ostensibly Kunti and Draupadi, but Satyavati's stature is far from negligible. She changes the very course of the Kuru dynasty because it is her pre-marital son, Krishna Dwaipayana or Vyasa, who fathers the future heirs to the throne of Hastinapura, thereby creating an eclectic intermingling of castes and classes. The war pivots around Draupadi as it is she who steadfastly keeps the fires of revenge burning for thirteen long years. Gandhari plays a significant role in her own way. While she fails in altering the course of events that lead to the Great War, she asserts herself forcefully at crucial moments. Finally, it is her curse that works itself out in the destruction of the Vrishnis and the ignominious death of Sri Krishna himself. But besides the five, there are several women who play very significant and key public roles on different occasions.

After the war, King Yudhishthira is persuaded to perform the Ashwamedha Yagna. After completing the due ceremonies, Sage Vyasa commands Arjuna to protect the horse and follow it to conquer the entire world while Bhima stays behind to protect the kingdom, and Nakula and Sahdeva to look after the guests. As Arjuna follows the steed, defeating any king who comes his way, a great battle occurs between him and the Saindhavas, who still live after the slaughter of their clan in Kurukshetra and are determined to avenge the killing of their King Jayadratha by Arjuna. Great destruction takes place and the Saindhavas begin to lose when Dushala, their queen, the daughter of Dhritarashtra and the widow of the slain Jayadratha, takes her infant grandson and meets Arjuna for the safety of all the Saindhava warriors. Weeping, she reminds Arjuna that the infant prince is his grandson as he is the son of Suratha, Jayadratha's son and hence is like Parikshit. Suratha, she tells him, died of grief on hearing how Arjuna had killed his father on the battlefield and on being once again confronted by an impending war. Dushala orders the Saindhavas to cease the battle and seeks Arjuna's protection, appealing for mercy.

Arjuna also goes to Gandhara and fights the ruler who is Shakuni's son. His mother is filled with fear and comes to meet Arjuna with all the aged ministers, forbidding her son to fight any more. Peace is established and for the sake of Dhritarashtra and Gandhari, Arjuna decides to spare the life of his counterpart in exchange for an oath to cease any future hostilities between them.

Men may think that they control these women. They try to bind them with moral codes or terrorize them into submission by threatening them with dire consequences and penalties for any transgression of the codes. Even so, these women know how to operate in a male-dominated world by subverting the male hegemony and inverting the *de jure* power structures to get *de facto* power in their own hands. Repeatedly, Kunti and Draupadi compel the men to act in ways that lead to crucial decisions at critical moments. Of course, they work largely through their husbands and sons (hence the pressure on each to produce the first son) and consequently, are unable to forge a solidarity or even friendship among themselves. This could explain the rivalry between Gandhari and Kunti, or between Kunti and Maadri. Gandhari is astute enough to know that the boon of a hundred sons is hollow if hers is not the first born, as at stake is the throne of Hastinapura. The importance of sons also determines the male attitudes towards female sexuality and gives the women immense power as wives and mothers because, after all, it is only they who can reproduce, making the power structures, both in the private and the public spheres, ambiguous.

Draupadi, however, is different from the other Kuru women and that is why she is an enigma. Born as an adult from the ritual fire, she is destined to be the cause of the destruction of thousands of Kshatriyas, according to the prophecy at her birth. Married to the five Pandavas, she is at once the equal of men and a challenge to the existing patriarchal norms. On several occasions, she protects her husbands and gives them sustenance and strength rather than being protected by them. It is no wonder that she is worshipped as Shakti in several temples devoted to Draupadi Amma in South India and even in places such as Reunion Island. Draupadi's power manifests itself in the cult of "fire walking" associated with her, widespread in Sri Lanka, Singapore, Malaysia, Reunion Island, Fiji and other places.

In evaluating the women's situation, we cannot conclude that they enjoy authority only because they are respected and worshipped as deities, mothers, sisters, wives, or daughters.

Women have always been respected in these roles, but it is a derived respect, a respect primarily accorded to roles they enjoy through their relationships with men. In such cases a woman is not seen as an individual on her own terms but derives her position through a man, a husband, a son, a father, or a brother. When women are defined through men, they may be respected but they are denied independent positions and voices. The *Mahabharata* itself makes a distinction between respect for self and the respect due to socially-given identities.

For example, when Garuda, flying with the Rishi Galava on his back, stops to rest on Mount Rishabha, the two are greeted by a young woman ascetic Sandili, who offers them food and rest. But on the following morning when they awake, Garuda finds that his wings have been clipped and that he has been reduced to a ball of flesh. Seeing his helpless condition, Rishi Galava asks him if he had entertained any sinful thoughts during the night. He replies that the only idea that had crossed his mind was that he should carry the ascetic Sandili from Mount Rishabha to where the divine Mahadeva and Vishnu, personifications of virtue and sacrifice, reside. He is now ready to prostrate himself before Sandili and ask for her pardon. Sandili tells him that by his thoughts he had entertained contempt for her. She had attained high ascetic success through the purity of her own conduct, that had led her to virtue and prosperity and driven away all that was inauspicious. She admonishes him never to be contemptuous of women even when they deserved blame. Saying this, she restores his wings along with his strength and energy.

In another instance, the female woman ascetic, Sulabha, chastises King Janaka, the great king of Mithila, for his claim that he is liberated and free from all attachments despite being the ruler of Mithila. She defeats him in knowledge, learning, and argument.

Both Sandili and Sulabha are ascetics and hence out of the

mainstream of society. So, does a woman have to renounce marriage and family and adopt the lonely path of asceticism to be independent and respected in her own right? Are single women an embarrassment as they are perceived to have unbridled sexuality that can be a threat to the order and discipline of society and so they need to be contained and institutionalized through systematic regulation? Not quite. There are queens like Hidimbi, Chitrangada, Ulupi, and others, popular in South India, like Alli, Pavazhakoddi, and Monnliyal, Arjuna's wives, who have autonomy over their own lives and are not dependent on men for their position or protection. However, the attempt in the narrative is to somehow bring them into the folds of patriarchal norms. This is because of the interpolation of regional narratives with different values in the *Mahabharata* and their consequent transformations. They add new dimensions to the core story and provide a constant re-interpretation. Some, despite the passage of time, remain outside the patriarchal mainstream of the *Mahabharata,* others become a part of it, while still others incorporate both matriarchal and patriarchal values.

The residue of matrilineal norms is perceived in the instance of Bhishma having to pay a bride price for Maadri in exchange for her marriage to Pandu. Many women, outside the pale of patriarchal norms, are characterized as demons or as celestial beings like *apsara*s. Hidimbi, for example, is a *rakshasa*, the sister of the demon, Hidimba, the ruler of the forest, and Urvashi who curses Arjuna is an *apsara*, who is powerful enough to turn him into a neuter at least for a year.

The *Mahabharata* acknowledges the power that resides with women. It is felt that they must be dealt with if state power itself is to be preserved. Therefore Yudhishthira, the newly anointed king after the war, requests Bhishma, lying on his bed of arrows, to tell him about the disposition of women who are supposed to be the root of all evil and are regarded as exceedingly frail. Marriage, motherhood, and family are considered sacrosanct. The well-being of society depends on women and hence of the state. If the norms pertaining to them are threatened and challenged, the order of life quickly degenerates into chaos.

Women's sexuality is seen as potentially an extremely destructive force in front of which the mightiest of men are rendered helpless. Yet, it can be put the great use once it is subordinated and regulated. Hence, women are divided into two classes: the utterly destructive because of their unbridled sexuality and the chaste wives and mothers. Within this polarity lie the ambiguities of *niyoga* or levirate, polyandry, and a woman's freedom to take the initiative in approaching a man. There are also ambivalences regarding the relationship between the wife and the husband's brother. All these indicate the changing social structures at different points of time as the *Mahabharata* evolved for about a thousand years before reaching its present from. It also shows variations of region, class, and caste. On the one hand it is legitimate to forcibly abduct a woman for marriage but on the other hand, a woman has the freedom to reject a suitor at her *swayamvara* in spite of being bound by conditions laid down by her male relatives, as Draupadi abjures Karna.

Yudhishthira's question possibly brings Bhishma face-to-face with his own pent-up anger and frustrations at the various turns of his life because of one word given to a woman. He is at loss for an answer and so does not give a direct reply. He prevaricates and recounts the discourse between Narada and the celestial courtesan, Panchachuda, to formulate his answer. He uses the agency of Panchachuda to denounce women in the strongest possible terms. Women are the cause of all sin, extremely lascivious, and always ready to bestow favours on any man who comes their way even if he is an invalid or an idiot. They cannot be restrained by the Creator himself says

Bhishma. He cites the Rishi Devasarman's words to his disciple, Vipula. According to the Rishi, there are two classes of women: those who are virtuous and those who are not. The virtuous women are the highly blessed mothers of the universe who uphold the earth with all its waters and forests. They need to be protected and cherished. Those who are not virtuous employ their unbridled sexuality through which they destroy the entire race and cannot be restrained or protected.

Bhishma explains this division. There was a time when women were as virtuous as men and therefore, were equally eligible for the status of deities. This alarmed the gods who went to Brahma for help as they did not wish to lose their superior position in the hierarchy of creation. Brahma then created women with the aid of Atharvan rites and implanted in them at the time of their creation the desire for the enjoyment of all kinds of carnal pleasure. Thus, those who were created from illusion became sinful while the others remained chaste. Brahma then created wrath as the companion of lust and men yielding to the power of both desired women intemperately, causing evil.

From a patriarchal point of view, the mightiest of men can be manipulated through sexual desire and the overpowering force of women's sexuality. The only way out to subordinate women and regulate their conduct is by controlling their sexuality in the garb of morality and virtue. Chastity in the context of the *Mahabharata* does not mean fidelity to one man. If the sexual conduct of a woman is controlled by a man, it allows for the ambiguities of *niyoga* or levirate, polyandry, a woman's freedom to take initiative, forcible abduction of a woman for marriage as in the case of Subhadra by Arjuna with the active connivance of Sri Krishna, her brother, and the right of a woman to reject a suitor despite being bound by conditions laid down by the father. These variations are all possibly indicative of the changing social structures and the *Mahabharata* absorbing within itself variations in time and region and consequently social structures and ethical norms.

Questions arise. Why is Bhishma so bitter about women? Is it because he feels that he has never received any love or care from them? Right from his infancy, his mother Ganga first deprives him of paternal love by taking him away from his father and then of maternal love in his adolescence as she sends him back to his father but keeps herself away. Or is it because of his disgust and anger at having been forced to give up the throne and his right to have children only because of his father's dotage over a young fisher girl, remaining oblivious of all the repercussions? After all, his father's turbulent passion for Satyavati utterly ruins Bhishma's life forever. Or is it years of suppressed anger because of the unjust sacrifice demanded of him that makes him adhere to his vow when not only has it lost all relevance but has also become dysfunctional? His adherence to it has consistently put Hastinapura in danger of being left without an heir. Suppression of all emotions and natural desires makes him the ultimate misogynist. While very obviously and extremely disturbed at the turn of events and while repeatedly appealing to Dhritarashtra to stop the most unacceptable and unprecedented humiliation taking place, he ultimately remains a distraught but mute spectator when Draupadi is disrobed in the court of Hastinapura. Even when she appeals to him, he can only say ineffectually that dharma is very subtle and confusing and hence he can do nothing; he merely hangs down his head in shame.

But such a dharma, is an empty shell and the answer of the great patriarch of the Kuru line only mirrors his moral confusion both in the private and the public domains. Despite having given up the throne of Hastinapura, he is fiercely attached to it. He remains its virtual ruler through the reigns of Vichitravirya and Chitrangada and then after their early deaths, through the growing up of Dhritarashtra and Pandu. The intense attachment with which he clings to Hastinapura can be seen from his tolerance of Duryodhana's machinations to eliminate the Pandava brothers through drowning, poisoning, and burning. He concomitantly watches helplessly the honour of the Kuru household being sullied in the Hastinapura court when one brother publicly molests another brother's wife. Finally, he fights on the wrong side knowing full well that he is doing so. Perhaps that is why he is made to lie on the bed of arrows, as much a psychological metaphor as it is physical, when he must confront and resolve every motivation of his mind and the ambiguities of his actions with their consequences on others at every turn of his life, before he can attain salvation and peace.

The *Mahabharata*, through Bhishma's discourse and events of the narrative, portrays a patriarchal structure that is also hierarchical, and these two paradigms operate in many layers of complexity both in the public and the private spheres. In the public sphere the hierarchical structure is seen in the superiority of the two ruling classes — the Brahmins and the Kshatriyas, the scholars and the warriors, respectively — between whom, an equation must be established so that they do not challenge each other's hegemony and create conflict. Interestingly, this is done again through the agency of women. Parashurama, angered by the death of his father Rishi Jamadagni, sets out on a conquest of the world with the sole aim of exterminating Kshatriyas. When he has annihilated all of them, the Kshatriya women approach the Brahmin men to beget offspring from them. These are regarded as virtuous motives and hence no sin accrues to them. Thus, the Kshatriya race is revived, and the Kshatriyas and Brahmins get related by ties of blood. A division of functionality is established between them so that both requirements of governance can be fulfilled: rule by sagacity and action through war. These two get intermingled in Drona, a warrior Brahmin who, insulted by Drupada, avenges himself by obtaining half his kingdom through Arjuna, as *gurudakshina*, and rules over it.

Within the patriarchal framework women are considered chaste and acquire that status not necessarily through fidelity to one man but by allowing their sexuality to be regulated by men, as wives or as daughters. It is customary, for example, for heirless kings to invite Brahmins to their house to seek their favour and blessings for sons. The daughters of the house serve them, looking after all their needs and even share their bed if they so desire, to please them. Kunti, as the young Pritha, is thus appointed by her adoptive father Kuntibhoja to look after Durvasa Rishi, who, pleased by her conduct, bestows on her a mantra by which she can call upon any man or god as she may desire. Gradually, as Pandu later explains to Kunti, the scope of chastity has got progressively narrowed as patriarchy has gradually become more firmly entrenched. This is done by Swetaketu, the son of Rishi Uddalaka. However, Swetaketu also makes it imperative upon men to treat chaste and loving wives well otherwise they are guilty of sin. Further, he prohibits women from begetting offspring from other men, even at the behest of their husbands.

The sexuality of women has to be controlled and the position of a chaste wife needs to be given primary importance as no family can come into existence without her. She is seen to be vital for bringing forth the much-needed sons and for making a home. Her primary duty is obedient service to the husband. Since marriage is sacred, taking place before the holy fire and the husband is the wife's highest deity, her whole being should be devoted to pleasing him.

The duties of a chaste wife are expounded repeatedly in the *Mahabharata*. As is the usual technique in the epic, different characters are used to say the same thing in different situations to lay down the dharma or the moral principle. Sandili tells Sumana the duties of a chaste wife. Parvati lays down the code of conduct for herself at the behest of Mahadeva who assures her that it would become universal law since she forms half the part of his body. The duties of a woman, says Uma, are created through kinsmen in the rites of marriage. In the presence of the mystical fire, a woman become the associate of her husband in the performance of all righteous deeds. This makes her equal partner of her husband. It is not clear whether a woman has the right to dissociate herself from the unrighteous actions of her husband. The question is not far removed from the issue raised by Draupadi after the game of dice, whom did Yudhishthira lose first, himself or his wife, Draupadi herself. It foregrounds the whole question of the status of a wife and the extent of her husband's rights over her.

However, all the obligations are not on the wife alone. Within this framework, some space has been created for a wife's rights. When a chaste wife deviates, the fault is of the husband. For example, Gautama orders his son Chirkari to kill his mother as she transgresses the dharma. He then leaves for the forests. Chirkari is caught between following is father's orders as a son and his duty to protect his mother. He decides to follow the latter, arguing that when a husband does not remain a provider or a protector, he loses the privileges accruing to him. In the meantime, Gautama realizes his error and rushes back to prevent the killing of his wife from being carried out. He blesses his son for disobeying him and realizes that in worldly affairs it is not prudent to take decisions in haste or anger.

The learned but blind Dirghatamas, acquires a young and beautiful wife, Pradweshi. Realizing the legitimacy of the practice of *niyoga*, he enters other carnal relationships, beyond the limits of propriety. The other *muni*s get indignant and cast him off. His wife is dissatisfied with him and asserts that she will not support him as she has done so far. A husband is called 'bhartri' (supporter) because he supports a wife and is a 'pati' because he protects her. Since he has failed in both the roles, she, his wife, cannot be expected to look after him any longer. The *Mahabharata* presents a galleria of women. Their words and actions make them the driving force behind the men. They constantly intervene, manipulate, subjugate, and subvert to make a place for themselves and to exercise power. The men think they control them and are superior to them, but these are intelligent, brave, and beautiful women who can neither be brow-beaten nor subdued.

2

___

SATYAVATI AND AMBA

SATYAVATI

This queen of the *Mahabharata* comes like a storm to Hastinapura. According to the conditions set by her foster father, no doubt with her acquiescence, her sons from Shantanu will ascend the throne of Hastinapura rather than the rightful heir Devavrata, the son of Shantanu and Ganga. This turns Devavrata into Bhishma, or the taker of the terrible vow. His father's state of love sickness moves him to pledge, not only to renounce the throne of Hastinapura, but also promise never to marry and have children to eliminate even the possibility of a threat to Satyavati's children from his side. Devavrata's sacrifice parallels that of another of his ancestors, Puru. This is a typical narrative technique of the *Mahabharata*: an issue is examined from different angles by narrating tales at various points in the text showing several different situations that may arise out of it.

Puru the fifth and the youngest son of Yayati, is one of the great ancestors of the Pandavas, a renowned ruler devoted to his subjects and a brave warrior. Yayati becomes prematurely old, cursed for having wronged his wife Devyani, by her father

Shukracharya who is a highly respected preceptor. He laments that he has not yet satiated his desires and is still haunted by his sensual passions. He wants to satisfy them but can only get back his youth if one of his sons exchanges his youth for the father's old age. Each one of his first four sons declines, but the youngest son, Puru, gladly makes the exchange. Puru becomes old and rules the kingdom wisely, while Yayati enjoys life and even goes to the garden of Kubera to sport for several years with an *apsara*. Eventually, he realizes the futility of trying to quench or fulfil desire because it was like fire, the more it is fed, the more it blazes. It is only equanimity of the mind that brings peace and hence Yayati once again takes back his old age from his son Puru, while returning him his youth, and retires to the forests.

This lesson is learnt the hard way repeatedly. The futility of Devavrata's renunciation is borne out by the subsequent course of events. Satyavati, on whose behalf the promise had been extracted from him, finds herself prematurely childless and Hastinapura without an heir. She is forced to plead with that very person whom she had tried to exclude from the throne earlier, to father an heir through a levirate relationship with her daughters-in-law, Ambika and Ambalika, widows of her son Vichitravirya. Bhishma, smouldering with subconscious anger at the magnitude of the injustice done to him by the reckless desire of his father, adheres stubbornly to a now empty and futile vow. Instead, he persuades Satyavati to look for another suitable person for this purpose. A stunning piece of news is then given to him. He is after all irrelevant because Satyavati, who had demanded life-long celibacy from him, herself has a premarital son before her marriage to Bhishma's besotted father, Shantanu. He is the great Rishi Vyasa, in a way his brother, and obviously the most suitable candidate for the purpose if Bhishma refuses to budge from his resolve. The consequence, however, is that not a drop of Shantanu's blood now runs in the veins of the future kings of Hastinapura and the Chandravanshi dynasty, in effect, comes to an end. What remains is only a *de jure* clan, whether it is the Kauravas or the Pandavas, who finally ascend the throne of Hastinapura.

Satyavati's birth is an unusual and dramatic as her life. This is a device used to indicate the out-of-mould character of the women whether it is Draupadi born from fire or Kunti given away in her infancy by her parents to Surasena, her father Kuntibhoj's childless cousin and friend. Brought up by the chief of fishermen, Satyavati is in fact the daughter of King Uparichara, a Vasu, and the apsara or celestial maiden Adrika, but this is not known to him. One day, Uparichara goes to slay a deer at the command of his ancestors, or *pitris*, leaving his young and beautiful newly married wife Girika behind. In the forests, maddened by the spring fragrance of flowers, he cannot keep his thoughts away from his lovely wife and so asks a hawk to carry his seed to her. On the way, the hawk is pursued by another hawk who thinks the former is carrying meat; in the ensuing fight, the seed drops into the water of Yamuna where it is swallowed by Adrika, who has been transformed into a fish because of a Brahmin's curse. Adrika as a fish gives birth to twins, a boy and a girl, whom the wonderstruck fisherman takes to his king, Uparichara. The king adopts the boy who later became the virtuous and honest monarch, Matsya, but he gives the girl away to the chief of fishermen to be raised by him as his daughter. She grows up to be a beautiful and intelligent young lady with only one problem – she has a fishy odour that emanates from her body because of her birth and continued contact with fishermen. Adrika, meanwhile, freed of her curse resumes her celestial shape.

The irony of fate is that Satyavati, who is a king's daughter, is brought up by a fisherman. She is unknowingly given away by her own father even after she is brought by the fisherman to his house, as an infant. As Satyavati grows up, she plies a boat on the waters of the River Yamuna to help her foster father. One day, Rishi Parashara sees her, and on beholding her, he cannot contain his desire for her. Being persuaded by him, she gives in but on the condition that she will be rid of the fishy smell and that her body will henceforth have a sweet fragrance that can be smelt for one *yojana* (a measure of distance, equalling 12-15 km).

The Rishi delightedly not only bestows her with the sweet irresistible fragrance but also promises Satyavati that she will regain her virginity after their union. For her bodily fragrance, Satyavati also acquires the names of Gandhavati and Yojana-gandha. Later, her fragrance lures Shantanu to her and on witnessing her bewitching beauty, he is maddened with desire and wishes to marry her.

Sage Parashara then creates a mist around them on the boat as he unites with Satyavati and because of the coupling, a son is born to her on an island where she goes for childbirth. Since he is dark-complexioned, he is called Krishna, or the dark one, and being born on an island, he is known as Dwaipayana or the island-born. Krishna Dwaipayana sets his mind on asceticism with his mother's permission becomes the most learned of men who grows up to be known as Vyasa, or the arranger of the Vedas and the author of the fifth Veda or the *Mahabharata,* that he writes for the education of the masses who do not otherwise have access to the wisdom of the Vedas. He is also its chief protagonist as later it is his grandchildren, the Kauravas and the Pandavas, who fight the great *Mahabharata* war.

Krishna Dwaipayana goes away promising his mother that he will come to her whenever she remembers him. True to his word he arrives in Hastinapura when Satyavati calls upon him to father the future kings of Hastinapura from her two daughters-in-law, Ambika and Ambalika, widows of his half-brother Vichitravirya. Thus, Satyavati ensures that Hastinapura has an heir but having done that she does not cling to the throne like

Bhishma. Warned by her son Sage Vyasa that her progeny will fight a suicidal war, she takes his advice and retires to the forests together with her daughters-in-law rather than witness the carnage that is destined to follow.

AMBA

Ambika and Ambalika have an elder sister Amba, who is also forcibly abducted by Bhishma along with them. While they are married to Vichitravirya, Amba becomes a symbol of revolt. Bhishma narrates her story to Duryodhana as they take stock of the warriors on either side before the war. Bhishma talks of the great warrior Sikhandin against whom he will not take up arms no matter what the provocation, as he is born a woman who has later become a man. Bhishma maintains that it is beneath his honour to fight women. What could have brought about such a transformation? Is it the unequal patriarchal society with its norms where men fail to protect a woman but do not hesitate to unjustly ruin her life blinded because of their own pretty egos and vanities? Or is it necessary to experience life both as man and a woman to completely understand the pain of humanity? Is that why later, the greatest of bowmen and warriors, Arjuna lives the life of a woman for a year in King Virata's household and be known as a eunuch?

After Shantanu's death, Bhishma installs his half-brother Chitrangada on the throne in keeping with his vow. Chitrangada dies early fighting a Gandharva and so Bhishma crowns Chitrangada's child brother, Vichitravirya, the king in accordance with Satyavati's wishes. Not only does Bhishma install him as king, but he also sets about obtaining brides for him. To that end, Bhishma goes to Kasi, where the king has organized a *swayamvara* for his three beautiful daughters — Amba, Ambika, and Ambalika. All the kings have assembled for the occasion. Bhishma goes there and, challenging all the assembled kings, forcibly abducts all the three princesses in his chariot. A massive fight ensues between Bhishma and the princes gathered there, but the former singled-handedly and easily vanquishes them all, including Salva to whom Amba has secretly given her heart, and returns to Hastinapura. He places the three girls in Satyavati's care to be married to Vichitravirya. Satyavati is overjoyed but Amba protests to Bhishma saying that she is already emotionally committed to the King of Salvas. He, too, had approached her privately before the *swayamvara* without her father's knowledge. She is confident that Salva will be expecting her and therefore Bhishma should permit her to go to him. On hearing this, Bhishma consults Satyavati, the priests, and the counsellors and decides to send Amba to the King of Salvas with all respect due to her. Salva, however, refuses to accept her and tells her to return to Bhishma as she has been sullied by having been forcibly taken away by him. Amba's anxious pleas saying that he is being unjust; that she did not go voluntarily; and her assurances that Bhishma has not even touched her, are of no avail.

Evidently, Salva's false sense of pride makes it impossible for him to reconcile to his failure to prevent Bhishma from carrying away Amba in his very presence. His hurt ego does not allow him to see how unreasonable and unjust he is being. Perhaps he also fears Bhishma's anger by now accepting Amba whom Bhishma has 'won'. Bhishma's invincibility and ability to punish by force of arms is well known. Salya now finds a convenient excuse to escape a difficult situation while keeping face and shifting the blame elsewhere.

Angry and rejected, Amba blames Salva for spurning her, her father for arranging a *swayamvara* in a manner from which she could thus be easily abducted, herself for not having had the courage to jump out of Bhishma's carriage, but most of all, she blames Bhishma for causing her the plight. She realizes that she can neither go back to her father's house nor to Hastinapura, as she left from there only to marry Salva who has now betrayed her. She knows that no ruler on earth will venture to fight with Bhishma.

Here, there are minor variations to the story. In one version, Amba returns to Hastinapura, where Bhishma tries to persuade Vichitravirya to marry her who refuses because he knows, that she already belongs to another person. Amba then turns to Bhishma and begs him to marry her himself. This, of course, he cannot do, and he thus persuades her to return to Salva once again. For the second time Salva spurns her. By now, six long years have passed and Amba's suffering knows no end. She then decides to go to the forests to do penances to become capable of taking revenge on Bhishma. In another version she immediately goes to the forests after being rebuffed by Salva and tells the great ascetics dwelling there, of her plight.

At this point again, there are at least two versions to the tale, but they do not functionally change the course of events. Amba observes hard austerities in the forests when Lord Subrahmanya appears before her and gives her a garland of ever-fresh lotuses, saying that the wearer of that garland would become the enemy of Bhishma. Amba takes the garland and appeals to every Kshatriya to accept it and champion her cause. But who dares to fight Bhishma? Finally, she goes to King Drupada who also refuses her prayer. She then hangs the garland on Drupada's palace gate and goes away to the forest.

In an ashrama in the forest lives an eminent ascetic, Saikhavatya, who asks her what she wants. Amba expresses her desire to live in the forests as she has renounced the world and that she wants to practice the severest ascetic austerities. She feels that her sufferings are because of sins that she may have committed in a former life, out of ignorance. She wants to be instructed in ascetic penance and the sage Saikhavatya promises help.

The other ascetics try to dissuade Amba from choosing the

harsh life of the forests as she is a delicate princess, and they advise her to return to her father's home. A woman, who does not have a husband as her protector in harsh times, should be protected by her father, they say. Also, alone in the woods, a princess of her beauty and tenderness is not safe as kings could come to court her and that would lead to strife. Of course, the underlying motive for this advice can also be that such a situation will jeopardize their peaceful existence.

Amba knows that there is no place for her in her father's home and is determined to survive the rough practice of austerities so that she does not have to suffer in the future. While the sages are still debating the further course of action, Amba's maternal grandfather, Hotravahana, arrives. When he hears the entire saga, he consoles his granddaughter but also becomes immensely anxious for her. He feels that the best thing for her is to go to Parashurama (Rama), the son of Jamadagni, and say that she has been sent by him to seek his help; only he can challenge and slay Bhishma. While they are talking thus, Akritavarna, a dear companion of Rama, arrives and announces that Rama himself will be there the following day. Hotravahana then tells him Amba's entire history.

Akritavarna asks Amba what she wants — to marry Salva or to see Bhishma defeated. She leaves the best course of action to Akritavarna who, after evaluating the situation, concludes that there is really no hope of Salva accepting her after she had been carried off by Bhishma. Hence, Bhishma is the actual cause of her misery and so her vengeance must be directed towards him. Amba agrees and wishes to be the cause of Bhishma's death in a battle.

When Rama comes the following day, Hotravahana, after the initial pleasantries, tells him of his granddaughter Amba's plight. Amba also pleads with him and seeks his help. He promises to ask Bhishma to marry her; if Bhishma refuses then, he assures them, he will consume him in battle. He says that if

Amba desires, he can even address the king of Salva. After narrating the entire sequence of events to him, she says that she will, of course, follow whatever the sage decides for her, but she feels that since Bhishma is the root cause of her suffering by the violent abducting, he should be slain.

Rama says that he no longer takes up arms from his own desire after the carnage he caused in destroying the Kshatriyas; but he does so only on behalf of those conversant with the Vedas. However, he is confident that since both Bhishma and Salva are obedient to him, he will be able to solve Amba's problem. Rishi Akritavarna reminds him that after his war with the Kshatriyas, while he has vowed to fight only with those who are foes of the Brahmins, he has also promised not to abandon those who come to him for protection. Hence, it is his duty to battle Bhishma. Rama, however, wants conciliation and so he goes to Bhishma accompanied by Amba and others from the Ashrama.

Hearing that sage Parashurama has come to their kingdom, Bhishma goes respectfully to meet him. Rama reiterates that having abducted Amba, it is Bhishma's duty to marry her. However, Bhishma explains that he acted only on behalf of Vichitravirya, and at Amba's request, had sent her to Salva with all due respect and honours. He himself is bound by a vow of celibacy that he cannot abandon, come what may. Despite Rama's repeated pleadings, Bhishma remains firm in his resolve; this enrages Rama. Bhishma, too, gets angry as he feels that Rama, his preceptor, is being unreasonable. Left with no choice, Bhishma reluctantly decides to fight Rama on the battlefield of Kurukshetra. Both proceed there. Bhishma narrates everything to Satyavati and prepares for battle. Just then Ganga, his mother, appears and tries to dissuade him. She says that she herself will request Rama to desist from fighting. Bhishma tells her all about Amba, and Ganga goes to Rama, who insists that the only way out is for Bhishma to do his bidding regarding Amba. Ganga too tries to persuade her son but Bhishma refuses. There is no option left but for the two of them to settle matters on the battlefield.

The battle between Rama and Bhishma carries on for several days. On the fourth day, Bhishma's charioteer gets killed. While Bhishma is grieving over his loss, Rama wounds him with his arrows and he falls to the earth, bloodstained and in a swoon. Rama thinks he is dead. Together with Akritavarna, Amba and others, he is overjoyed, but eight Brahmins mysteriously appear. They surround Bhishma as he is falling and hold him before his body can touch the ground. They revive him with words of encouragement and his mother Ganga now takes command of his steeds as his charioteer. However, Bhishma worships her and respectfully assuring her that he can manage by himself, requests her to leave. He takes charge of his chariot and fights once again.

As the battle remains indecisive day after day, the eight Brahmins, who revived Bhishma, appear to him in a dream and give him a weapon of great destruction, the Prasvapa. Seeing his hesitation on using this weapon on his preceptor and incurring the sin of his death, they assure him that no fault will attach to him as he himself would both vanquish and raise Rama. The following day, when the battle rages in all its intensity, Bhishma finally decides that to use the weapon. Ganga intervenes and stands between the two to call a halt to the destruction. The Brahmins also appear in the skies and asked Rama to desist.

Thus, after several days, the battle ends, Rama being asked by his ancestors to desist and Narada and Ganga asking Bhishma to stop. Conceding defeat, Rama tells Amba that she is free to chart out her own course of action. He realizes that Bhishma is invincible in battle. Amba thanks Rama for having tried his best on her behalf but she does not give up. Since Bhishma cannot be defeated by anyone, she decides to follow the ascetic path, determined to obtain the power to vanquish him herself. Rama returns to the mountains from where he had come and Bhishma informs Satyavati of all that has happened. He also sends spies to keep track of Amba's actions. When he finds out about the severe penances that she is putting herself through, he loses all joy in his victory and becomes very melancholy. He can foresee his end and tells both Narada Muni and Sage Vyasa that he is convinced that no amount of individual endeavour can overcome destiny.

Meanwhile, Amba remains engaged in her ascetic practices. Ganga comes to her one day and asks her why she is afflicting herself thus. Amba answers that since Bhishma vanquished Rama, no other king will now dare to challenge or fight him. Therefore, she is determined to gain the power herself to destroy him. Ganga, worried for her son Bhishma, curses her saying that she is acting crookedly and that her wish will never be fulfilled. Also, if she leaves her body while practicing these austerities, she will become a river in her next birth, crooked in course with water only during the rains. She will be dry for eight months; all the bathing places on her course will be difficult to approach; and she will be full of alligators and all kinds of frightful creatures. Amba thus becomes a rain river in Vatsabhumi but because she of ascetic merit she gains, only half of her body becomes such a river; the other half remains that of a maiden.

The ascetics in Vatsabhumi also try to dissuade Amba but undeterred and firm in her resolve, she carries on with a single-minded purpose. Eventually, her immense efforts bear fruit. Shiva appears before her and grants her the boon that she will slay Bhishma in her next life. When she asks him how that will be fulfilled as she is a woman, Shiva says that a boon once granted by him must fructify; although she will be reborn a woman, she will attain manhood after a period. She will remember the incidents of her past life even after getting a new body. Born in the race of Drupada, she will become a *maharathi* (great warrior), well-skilled in the use of weapons and in the art of warfare. On getting this boon from Shiva, Amba makes a funeral pyre and self-immolates. Having got what she wants in this life, living any further is a waste as far as she is concerned. She does not wish to lose any more time to take the next step.

Events close in on Bhishma. Drupada is childless. He venerates Shiva to get an offspring who will be the cause of Bhishma's death as he must avenge himself. He, therefore, wants a son not a daughter. Shiva tells him that he will have a child who would first be a female and then become a male. Drupada relates all this to his wife, Prishita. When the time comes, Prishita conceives and in due time gives birth to a beautiful daughter. She, however, lets it be known that a son has been born and all the rituals are performed accordingly. Drupada, keeping in mind the prophecy of Shiva, also falls in with his wife's plans. He publicly calls her Sikhandin (instead of Sikhandini, which is her name) and announces to the world that he has a son. No one, besides Drupada and his wife know the truth, except Bhishma, who is aware of Amba's asceticism and Shiva's boon.

Drupada educates Sikhandini very carefully. She learns from Drona and so has the same teacher as the Kauravas and the Pandavas. However, she remains a girl and grows up to be a woman. When she comes to a marriageable age, Drupada's wife urges her husband to find a wife for her. Drupada is worried, but Prishita is confident that Shiva's words cannot be false and hence there is no danger in continuing with this deception. The daughter of a powerful monarch, Hiranyavarman, the king of Dasarnakas, is chosen. After the marriage, the bride realizes that Sikhandini is actually a woman and confides this to her nurses who convey the truth to Hiranyavarman. Enraged, Hiranyavarman sends emissaries to Drupada to privately convey to him that he is determined to kill him for the deceit and for ruining his daughter's life.

Drupada knows that he is at fault and is naturally extremely fearful. He consults his wife and sends envoys to the ruler of Dasarnakas. He impresses upon his wife the danger to both Sikhandini and himself from which even she will not escape. He speaks to her in the presence of others to make them aware of his innocence and how he acted at the behest of his wife. Drupada also takes advice from his ministers and together they begin to prepare to protect the city from the impending invasion. In the meantime, Sikhandini is filled with shame and resolves to end her life. She goes into a thick and dark forest, the haunt of a formidable Yaksha, Sthunakarna. No one ever enters this forest for fear of him. She finds a mansion there and begins to practice penances and austerities. Moved, the Yaksha Sthuna appears and asked her the cause of her distress, with a promise to help. She narrates her tale and appeals for protection for herself and for her parents.

The Yaksha decides to give her his manhood for a certain period. For that while he is ready to take on her femaleness. He makes her promise that at the end of the stipulated time, she will return his manhood to him. Thus, she can save the city, her parents, and herself. Sikhandini agrees and thus the two exchange their sexes. Now a man, Sikhandin enters the city in great joy and tells Drupada all that has transpired. Drupada and Prishita are overjoyed and Drupada sends word to Hiranyavarman that he has been mistaken and misinformed and that Sikhandin is definitely a man. Hiranyavarman dispatches several beautiful young women to Sikhandin to find out the truth for himself and they all came back and report that he is a male. The king is delighted and after spending some time with Drupada, departs.

Meanwhile, Kubera, or Vaisravana, the lord of the Yakshas, who is always borne on the shoulders of human beings during his journey through earth, arrives at the abode of Sthuna. He finds everything beautiful while staying there but is upset that Sthuna himself is not attending on him. The other Yakshas explain that Sthuna is embarrassed because he has changed his sex and is now a woman. When he is summoned, Sthuna stands shamefully before Kubera, who is enraged and curses him that from then onwards he will always remain a woman.

At this, all the other Yakshas plead with Kubera to limit this curse. Eventually, Vaisravana agrees that Sthuna will regain his manhood after Sikhandin's death. Meanwhile, Sikhandin keeps to his word and returns to Sthuna as soon as Hiranyavarman leaves. Sthuna is pleased with him and narrates how he himself has been cursed. He advises Sikhandin to go and live peacefully with his people as the whole event had been pre-ordained. Thus Sikhandini, first born a woman transforms into a man, Sikhandin. Amba, the eldest daughter of the king of Kasi, finally succeeds in taking her revenge on Bhishma even if it takes her two lives to do it. She overcomes all the obstacles that cross her path and when everything and everyone fail her, she obtains the capacity to bring about the downfall of the great warrior Bhishma through her own grit and determination.

3

GANDHARI AND KUNTI

Kunti and Gandhari, wives of Pandu and Dhritarashtra respectively, are rivals for power and influence in the court of Hastinapura, as are their husbands for its throne, despite Pandu's demise. Their position was first directly related to that of their husbands and now with their sons: hence the rivalry over the number and age of the sons. Kunti, or Pritha, is the most resolute and focused and all along she exerts a strong influence over the course of events. Maadri, Pandu's second wife, is the quintessential married woman dependent and forever in need of protection. Gandhari comes across as assertive but not usually effective.

GANDHARI

Gandhari's life is a tragic one. Despite being the queen of Hastinapura and the mother of a hundred sons, she has virtually no say during events as they take place. But she evolves into a person with great inner strength and towards the end of her life, acquires the powers of an ascetic. She unfolds the blindfold momentarily and gazes on Duryodhana's naked body to make him into *vajra*, indestructible. Sages say that the power of her sight can do that. But again, this plan is foiled by Sri Krishna as he counsels Duryodhana that it is shameful for him to go stark naked in the presence of his mother. Duryodhana thus covers himself partially to the extent that his thighs remain vulnerable. One ray of light from her eye burns Yudhishthira's toenail. She curses Sri Krishna with the destruction of his clan, the Yadavas, and for him to die an ignoble death, for what she thinks was his devious role in the devastating war of *Mahabharata*.

Bhishma tells Vidura that there are only three princesses suitable for marriage in the Kuru family — Kunti, the daughter of Kuntibhoja, Maadri, the sister of King Salya, and Gandhari, the daughter of King Suvala of Gandhara. Consequently, he sends messengers with a proposal to King Suvala, for the marriage of Dhritarashtra and Gandhari. King Suvala is hesitant at first because he knows that Dhritarashtra is blind but considering the authority and fame of the Kurus he accepts the proposal. It is said that when Gandhari realizes that Dhritarashtra is blind but that her parents have accepted her marriage to him she, out of love and respect for her husband, blindfolds her eyes. But is this true? Isn't it the most illogical thing to do, to unnecessarily handicap herself and not even be able to help her husband? Does she do it because she feels helpless at not being able to assert herself and refuse this proposal in the manner that Draupadi does later and rejects Karna? Perhaps, driven by despair and anger, and to spite Bhishma, she decides to literally close her eyes to what is going on around her. She also becomes a living embodiment of the injustice of a patriarchal society in which she has been used merely as a tool to establish a useful political alliance through matrimony, notwithstanding that it shatters the natural dreams of a young girl on the threshold of marriage. There is nothing more left for her to see and the boon of a hundred sons can only mock her. Perhaps that is why there are two explanations as to how she even got this boon.

One explanation is that she got it from Shiva before her marriage and that can only be indicative of plenty and prosperity in marriage. Bhishma hears from some Brahmins that Gandhari, the daughter of King Suvala, is a great worshipper of Shiva and has obtained the boon from Shiva of a hundred sons. This information prompts him to plan the marriage between Gandhari and Dhritarashtra. In the second explanation, the boon is granted to her after her marriage. One day the great Krishna Dwaipayana comes to Gandhari's abode, exhausted with hunger and fatigue. She looks after him with such respectful attention that gratified with her hospitality, the Rishi grants her the boon that she asks for — that she should have a hundred sons each equal to her husband in strength and accomplishment. Does her insecurity with a blind husband, one who has been found unsuitable for the throne and whose authority is, therefore, always doubtful, make her ask for a hundred sons?

Gandhari conceives but carries the pregnancy for two long years without delivering. She then hears that Kunti has brought forth a son whose splendour is being likened to that of the morning sun. Being thus, the first-born son of the clan in the direct line of descent from Pandu, Yudhishthira is the obvious claimant to the throne of Hastinapura. Gandhari realizes that her boon of begetting a hundred sons is nothing but a mockery of her desire for a queen's grandeur. Impatient and angry, she strikes at her womb violently. Thereupon a hard mass of flesh, like an iron ball, comes out of her womb. Disgusted, she is about to throw it away when Dwaipayana, intuitively apprehending this impulsive act, suddenly appears. He expresses his shock at what she has done but Gandhari, equally in despair, explains her anguish to him. Sage Vyasa says that his words can never be futile. He promptly asks her to get a hundred pots filled with clarified butter and have them placed at a concealed spot. In the meantime, he orders that cold water be sprinkled on this ball of flesh. He divides the ball into a hundred and one parts, each about the size of a thumb. He instructs Gandhari to put these parts with great care into the pots for two years, after which, she should open the covers. Having thus made all the arrangements, he departs for the Himavat mountains to devote himself to asceticism. The hundredth-and-first part is, on Gandhari's request, a daughter, Dushala, providing some tenderness in an otherwise strife-filled existence in the Kuru court.

The full force of the harsh, indifferent, and cynical attitudes towards women at Hastinapura is thrown into relief in the episode marking the humiliation of Draupadi in the open court of Dhritarashtra, with all the elders witnessing the horrifying spectacle. It is Gandhari who finally comes to comfort Draupadi, pleading and stopping her in the nick of time from cursing the entire Kaurava clan. To signify this gross violation of all ethical norms, evil omens occur in the sacred chambers of worship at the palace. A jackal cries loudly and asses bray. Terrible birds answer their cries from all sides. Beholding these frightful auguries, Gandhari and Vidura protest and plead with the king to rectify matters as best as he can. Scared that some harm would come to him, Dhritarashtra upbraids Duryodhana. This is neither with repentance nor with any ethical consideration but only as an attempt to appease Draupadi and save himself from her wrath; he promises her any boon that she asks of him. It is only a cynical gesture on the part of Dhritarashtra to protect his power and safeguard his legitimacy; the humiliation of the daughter-in-law is no consequence.

Gandhari is usually never consulted or paid heed to, neither by her husband nor her sons. Yet she stands out as a magnificent character in her own right and rises to great moral heights. She is called upon to mediate and to instil some sense of decorum in Duryodhana when Sri Krishna arrives on his last peace mission before the war. When Duryodhana insults him in the court, Dhritarashtra senses the ill-boding. However, having no authority over his son, he only has Gandhari's wisdom and integrity to rely on to make the errant son realize that ethics and realpolitik demand patient consideration of Sri Krishna's proposals. If she can possibly pacify Duryodhana and make him rise above his blinding ego and vanity, then Sri Krishna's advice can still be taken, and a peaceful compromise reached.

Acting on Dhritarashtra's suggestion, Vidura brings Gandhari to the court. Dhritarashtra explains, in despair, that Duryodhana is defying all his commands and thus endangering both his sovereignty and life in his lust for the throne. So much so, he has hurriedly left the court with his counsellors in the middle of negotiations disregarding his superiors and dismissing the words of his well-wishers. Hearing this, Gandhari commands that Duryodhana be brought back to the court. In the meantime, she upbraids Dhritarashtra saying that he himself is to be blamed for Duryodhana's unacceptable behaviour because he has been too indulgent towards his son and has followed his wrong counsel. Duryodhana, by now, is completely overpowered by lust, arrogance, and anger and has become a slave to his delusion. Consequently, he cannot now be turned away from the path that Dhritarashtra himself has encouraged him to take. Why, she asks, has he been indifferent to the disunity that has become inevitable because of their actions, and the consequences of which were now staring them in their faces? Who indeed would choose to use force, she wonders, to overcome a crisis that can be resolved through conciliation, compromise, and gift?

Vidura, in the meantime, brings back a belligerent Duryodhana who, anticipating what his mother will say, comes in great anger, determined to have his way. Gandhari rebukes him and counsels him to listen carefully to what she has to say: If he makes peace, he will please Bhishma, both his parents and all his well-wishers, with Dronacharya at their head. Nobody can succeed in acquiring and keeping a kingdom following only his desires. In any case, a person who does not have his senses under control cannot enjoy sovereignty for any length of time. Lust and wrath are the arch enemies, and they deprive a man from possessing and enjoying his wealth and prosperity. Even if a kingdom can be won through wickedness, it cannot be retained. He who wishes to enjoy a long reign must understand both profit and virtue. Counsellors, too, cannot be kept in check by one who cannot restrain himself. Such a ruler is incapable of conquering his foes and so, is soon defeated and ruined. She advises unity with the Pandavas; all he needs to do is to give the Pandavas their due so that they can all rule happily; together enjoying the earth. There is no good to be derived from war and victory is never certain. Let not the earth be destroyed because of his arrogant stubbornness. Men can never acquire and retain wealth by avarice and so he must give up his greed and make peace with the Pandavas. Duryodhana rudely leaves the court yet again, disregarding his mother's advice and wise words of caution.

On his return from Hastinapura, Sri Krishna tells Yudhishthira all that transpired, including Gandhari upbraiding Duryodhana in front of the whole assembly. He narrates how she made it clear to her son that he and his counsellors are wicked. The kingdom of the Kurus is enjoyable only in due order of hierarchy and succession, she asserted. Duryodhana's unrighteousness will eventually destroy the kingdom. Dhritarashtra rules with the help of his advisor Vidura, who is a person of great foresight. However, even they are subordinate to Bhishma, who although having given up his right to the throne, is respected and revered as the eldest of them all. She explains how the kingdom went to Pandu rather than to Dhritarashtra who was the elder of the two because of his blindness but now Pandu's sons and grandsons have a right on it, especially so since Yudhishthira is the older of the two. This should be unequivocally proclaimed jointly by Bhishma, Dhritarashtra, and Vidura to remove any ambiguity and Yudhishthira should rule the kingdom, ably guided by the elders. Having reported all that transpired at the Kuru court, Sri Krishna concludes that he is convinced that Duryodhana will not yield, and that Yudhishthira has no option but to fight to gain the kingdom.

Gandhari watches helplessly as, one by one, her sons lose their lives in the battlefield. The worst blow for her is Duryodhana's death; and more devastating is to know that he is killed by Bhima through a clever ploy in violation of the rules of mace combat. It is significant, that the only person that Yudhishthira thinks of at that moment is Gandhari and he is filled with great fear. He knows that while she may not have had much say in the court and in the affairs of the state, she has observed severe ascetic austerities and has attained great spiritual heights; she has the power to consume the three worlds. He is too scared to confront her alone and face her to offer his condolences on her huge personal loss. He fears that when she hears that her son's death is consequent to an unworthy stratagem, she will reduce them all to ashes with the fire of her mind. Thinking thus, he pleads with Sri Krishna to go with him to console Gandhari and Dhritarashtra, who would also be there with her.

On reaching Hastinapura, Sri Krishna sees that Sage Veda Vyasa has already arrived there. He greets both the Sage and King Dhritarashtra and consoles the King saying that he must remember that Yudhishthira did try his best to live peacefully but was forced into war against his will by the actions of Duryodhana and Dhritarashtra himself. Yudhishthira tried his best for peace. He even went into exile. On the eve of the battle, he wanted only five villages as a peaceful alternative and Sri

Krishna himself tried to negotiate that peace agreement. However, afflicted by time and moved by avarice, as Sri Krishna points out, Dhritarashtra did not grant that request. It is undoubtedly his destiny, that has consistently made Dhritarashtra act unwisely in not overruling his son. The Pandavas cannot be blamed, asserts Sri Krishna. Dhritarashtra and Gandhari have no reason to hold malice towards the Pandavas and Sri Krishna assures them that Yudhishthira continues to have a lot of affection for them. He is grieved for them and, overcome with shame, has not had the courage to come before them.

Thereafter, Sri Krishna addresses the grief-stricken Gandhari. He tells her that there is no woman in the world who can equal her sagacity. He reminds her of the wise words that she spoke in the assembly, words filled with righteousness and which, if followed, would have been for the good of both sides. However, her sons did not obey her. She has always been courageous and ethical, rising above personal considerations and she refused to bless Duryodhana with victory. Knowing this, she should not now turn against the Pandavas. Sri Krishna knows that with the strength of her penances, she has acquired the capacity to destroy the whole earth and all the animate and inanimate creatures on it. He expresses his fear that she could misuse her powers and, on an impulse, end up doing something regretful. Gandhari acknowledges that her heart has been unsteady with grief but that his words have stabilized her. Having thus comforted Gandhari, Sri Krishna leaves hurriedly as he intuitively comes to know that Drona's son, Ashwatthama, is planning to cause great harm and destruction.

The war is over; the bodies of all the warriors lie strewn on the battlefield. Even before meeting Kunti, their own mother, the Pandavas go with Draupadi and Sri Krishna to see Gandhari who, although she does say to Sri Krishna in the first instance that his words have stabilized her, is immensely and deeply afflicted with grief on account of the death of her hundred sons. She wishes to curse Yudhishthira. Having fathomed the rage in her grief, Sage Vyasa warns her not to give way to her anger but instead to bring about healing through forgiveness. He cautions her against any rash act and like Sri Krishna, reminds her that Duryodhana, desiring victory, had pleaded with her on each of the eighteen days of the war to bless him with victory. And on each day, her only steady answer had been that victory will be where righteousness is. She must remember that her position is on the side of righteousness and accordingly, she must subdue her wrath.

Gandhari replies that she neither has any ill feelings towards the Pandavas nor does she wish them to perish. Her heart is agitated only because of the death of her sons. She also knows that she and Dhritarashtra now have a duty to protect and care for the Pandavas as much as Kunti does. She acknowledges that the Kauravas had been defeated and destroyed because of Duryodhana and Shakuni, and due to the actions of Karna and Duhshasana. The Pandavas are not at fault. She is not lamenting the consequences of the war but her deepest grievance is the unfair way in which Bhima killed Duryodhana, whom he could not have defeated in a just and fair combat.

On hearing Gandhari's words, Bhima confesses that he acted out of fear and to protect himself. He begs her forgiveness. He also acknowledges that she is right and that Duryodhana could not be slain in a fair and righteous battle and hence he took recourse to unrighteousness. But he states that he was forced into his action to prevent the greater destruction of dharma by the Kaurava brothers, who had deviated from ethical imperatives in every instance leading up to the war. Duryodhana was grossly unfair to Yudhishthira and deceitfully plotted to destroy the Pandavas on more than one occasion. He reminds her of the brutal and humiliating way Duryodhana insulted Panchali in the Kuru court. For that very act he surely deserved to be slain there and then but Yudhishthira restrained his brothers at the time. They waited patiently for thirteen years to get their due. Having won the war and slain Duryodhana, the hostilities on the two sides have come to an end.

Gandhari, whose extreme emotional despair is overwhelming, is not convinced. She argues that she and Dhritarashtra could have at least been left with one son, one who was not involved in deceit, for them to lean on in their old age. Yudhishthira approaches her, trembling, and with folded palms. He accepts, with guilt and grief, that he is the cause of the universal destruction and that she is fully justified in cursing him. Gandhari says nothing, but from behind the blindfold directs her eyes towards Yudhishthira's toe just as he is about to bend down in front of her to pay his respects. The force of the gaze burns the nail of his toe. Seeing this, Arjuna moves behind Sri Krishna and the other Pandava brothers become alarmed.

With her spiritual powers, Gandhari beholds the carnage of the battlefield. She can discern all the warrior heroes lying dead — her sons, Karna, her son-in-law Jayadratha, and Abhimanyu. She bewails their loss to Sri Krishna who is standing by her side; she points out the wailing Kuru women to him. Overwhelmed and distraught, she curses Sri Krishna since he is the only one, she asserts, who could really have prevented this war of annihilation and yet he allowed the destruction to take place. She curses him that thirty-six years from then, the Vrishni race will destroy itself and that he himself will die disgracefully in the wilderness.

On hearing Gandhari's words, Sri Krishna answers with a faint smile playing on his face — there is none in the world other than himself who can exterminate the Vrishnis, the Yadava clan, and that he has already set that process in motion. By her curse, she has only aided him in this task. The clan has become so powerful that they no one can slay them, be it human, god, or demon. This has made the Yadavas arrogant and sinful. They will, therefore, kill each other. Having humbly accepted the outcome of her grief and emotional outburst, he now firmly tells her to stop lamenting as this immense carnage has taken place because of her; her son, Duryodhana, was wicked, envious, and arrogant and instead of stopping him she encouraged him by omission, till it was too late. She could have been much more assertive and prevented her brother Shakuni and his machinations; she could have commanded him to leave Hastinapura, especially since she was aware of the negative effect that her brother was having on her son. Gandhari becomes very agitated on hearing these disagreeable words but Dhritarashtra, restraining himself, gets busy with Yudhishthira in putting the funeral arrangements in place.

Sometime after the war, Gandhari eventually proceeds to Vanaprastha with Dhritarashtra and Kunti, where they die together in a forest fire. However, much Sri Krishna may have belittled Gandhari's wrath and lament, her curse does not go in vain. He dies an ignominious death by the stray arrow of a hunter as he roams the forests alone, his kingdom having been destroyed and his race having perished.

KUNTI

Kunti is far more assertive than Gandhari and, unlike her, she is deeply entrenched in the power struggle. Her aim is to see her sons occupy the throne of Hastinapura and she guides them in every possible instance to help them achieve this. She shares several traits with her grandmother-in-law, Satyavati. Like her, she had an unusual childhood and a premarital son. Having married into the Kuru family, she firmly resolves to get her due of power and grandeur as a queen, notwithstanding the uncertainties of fate and the clamour of intrigue.

Born to Surasena, a Yadava chieftain and Vasudeva's father,

she is Vasudeva's sister and Sri Krishna's paternal aunt. Out of friendship and a former promise, Surasena gives her away to his childless cousin and friend Kuntibhoja, the son of his paternal aunt. As Kunti grows up, her foster father entrusts her the task of looking after the Brahmin guests that come to the household. The greatest challenge is the formidable Rishi Durvasa, who is known for his quick temper and propensity to curse without thinking. It was customary in those days for daughters of kings to be given such a responsibility, in fulfilling which, they were to refuse nothing to the guest. Well-pleased with Kunti's services and knowing, through his ascetic powers, the curse that was to befall Pandu, her future husband, he gives her a mantra or invocation by which she can summon any celestial being she likes and have a child by him.

After Durvasa leaves, Kunti is curious to find out whether the boon is real enough. She frivolously summons Surya, the sun god. As soon as she chants the mantra, that effulgent deity approaches her. Scared, Kunti explains that she was only testing the efficacy of the mantra, but Surya insists that if she does not accept his embraces, it will be a transgression on her part, which will have its consequences. He then cohabits with her, and a son is born bearing a natural gold armour and earrings, which are a part of the skin on the body. Like Satyavati did with sage Parashara, Kunti extracts from Surya the promise that her virginity will be restored to her after the birth of the child. However, unlike Satyavati, she cannot acknowledge her son publicly till it is far too late.

Kunti wonders sorrowfully of what she should do with her new-born son. Fear of relatives and social censure makes her cast him into the water. Fortunately, Radha and Aadhiratha of the *suta* caste find him, and bring him up as their own son. Hence, this son of Surya and Kunti grows up to be known Radheya, the son of Radha, and not Kaunteya, the son of Kunti. They named him Vasusena, or one born with wealth because of his natural gold armour and earrings. But he also gets known as Karna. Endowed with enormous strength, he grows up well skilled in the use of all weapons. He acquires widespread fame because of his generous spirit. No one returns empty-handed from him. He worships the sun and at that point of time there is nothing that he will not give away to any Brahmin who approaches him. His valour and skill make him a worthy rival to Arjuna and hence even the gods play foul with him. Indra, Arjuna's father, is worried about Radheya's powers and the consequences for Arjuna. One day Indra, disguises himself as a Brahmin approaches him. He asks Radheya for his natural armour and earrings. Knowing that acceding to this request could later prove fatal to him, and warned by Surya himself, Radheya still peels them off from his body with his sword and gives them to Indra as he does not want to turn down the request. This is what earns him the sobriquet, 'Karna', or the cutter or the peeler of his own armour. Indra, in return, gives him a powerful dart but says that it can only slay one person, whomsoever Karna chooses.

When Kunti, endowed with great beauty, virtue and accomplishment, comes of age, her foster father Kuntibhoja arranges her *swayamvara* to which he invites princes and kings of other countries for his daughter to select her husband. The intelligent Kunti sees Pandu, the king of Hastinapura, among the several princes', and places the nuptial garland around his neck. Although Pandu is the younger of the two Kaurava brothers, Dhritarashtra, the elder, has been disqualified from ascending the throne because he is blind. The irony is striking, because Pandu's reign is short-lived and Dhritarashtra, in effect, rules for practically his entire life. This establishes the dichotomy and the foundation for the future war of succession, because disqualifying Dhritarashtra does not mean that the claims of his sons can also be overlooked. The question, therefore, of who would succeed, the sons of the disqualified elder brother, or the sons of the enthroned younger brother Pandu, in the direct line of succession, was bound to acquire urgency as they grew up and needed to be resolved. The issue was complex. There was justification and validity on both sides and owing to such balanced stakes, the matter could either be resolved by the roll of a dice or by war, two equally fateful processes. It eventually resulted in the decisive *Mahabharata* war.

Sometime after Pandu's marriage to Kunti, Bhishma sets his heart upon getting him married a second time. With this intent, he goes to king Salya, and proposes marriage between his sister Maadri and Pandu. Here the remnants of matriarchy can be seen as Salya agrees but insists on an appropriate bride price, according to the customs of his family. Bhishma accepts this condition and on an auspicious day, Pandu is united with Maadri. Thus, another potentially disruptive factor in the line of succession to the throne of Hastinapura is added and Kunti acquires an immediate rival.

After a while, Pandu goes into the forests with his two wives to enjoy himself in a deer hunt. One day, while roaming on the southern slopes of Himavat, he chances upon a large stag coupling with his mate and goes on to shoot both with sharp arrows. This proves to be Pandu's undoing as the stag is really a rishi's son of great ascetic merit who chose to enjoy his mate in the form of a deer. The rishi curses Pandu that he will never be able to cohabit with a woman and if he tries, he will die. Overwhelmed with grief, Pandu decides to abdicate the throne and continue to live like an ascetic, in the forest.

The desire for a son, however, remains as Pandu fears that those without issues cannot be admitted into heaven and that if he has no son, his lineage will end. Incapable himself, he asks Kunti to obtain a son for him through a levirate relationship. After all he himself was born of such a union. At first, she is reluctant, but he convinces her. He tells her that this is accepted by the laws of dharma and enumerates twelve kinds of sons. The first six are accepted as heirs and the remaining six are not. Those who can inherit are: the son begotten on one's wedded wife; the son begotten upon one's wife by an accomplished person from motives of kindness; the son begotten on the wife after the husband's death; the maiden-born son, and one born of an unchaste wife. The latter six are: the son given; the son bought for a consideration; the son self-given; the son received with a pregnant bride; the brother's son; and the son begotten upon a wife of a lower caste. Event at this point Kunti does not reveal to him the fact of her premarital son, who according to the laws that Pandu himself has enumerated, could be a legal heir to Pandu. Why doesn't she? Perhaps because while this may have been valid by laws of kinship and succession, it would hardly be acceptable in the patriarchal society of Hastinapura and the Kauravas, especially when something as vital as the throne is at stake.

Pandu tries to further persuade Kunti by citing other precedents like that of the warrior daughter of Sardandayana who was asked by her husband to give him an offspring. With the help of a Brahmin ascetic, she had three sons who grew up to be mighty warriors, the eldest being Durjaya. But Kunti protests and says that she cannot even imagine another man's embraces. She then narrates the story of King Vyushitwasa, a great king in the race of Puru, and his wife Bhadra. Vyushitwasa dies prematurely of consumption much like Pandu's father Vichitravirya, but his corpse begets on his wife, seven children. Pandu, of course, is not willing to die in intercourse; ironically that is exactly how his life ends when he does not restrain himself with Maadri.

It is only after Pandu exhausts all his arguments and is desperately pleading with Kunti to bear him a son, that she tells him of Rishi Durvasa's boon, a mantra by which she can summon any celestial being she wants to give her a son. She consents to do Pandu a favour. This is superb power play. Having got the upper hand on him, she asks him to decide whom she should call first. He chooses Dharma, the god of justice and the most virtuous of the celestials. Kunti agrees and from him obtains a son, Yudhishthira. After Yudhishthira's birth, Pandu again asks his wife to obtain another son of superior strength. This time Kunti invokes Vayu, or the God of Wind. He gives her Bhima, a son of extraordinary strength, who is also known as Vikrodara or wolf belly.

After the birth of Vikrodara, Pandu concentrates on a son who would obtain worldwide fame. He wishes to get a son from Indra after pleasing him with his asceticism. He asks Kunti to also observe an auspicious vow for one year while he himself commences severe austerities and penances to gratify the lord of the celestials. After a long time, pleased by such devotion, Indra promises Pandu a son whose fame would spread over all the three worlds as a slayer of foes. Pandu then tells Kunti that Indra is willing to grant her a son of superhuman achievements, an oppressor of enemies, possessed of great wisdom and of great fame. He, therefore, begs her to invoke Indra. Thus, Kunti gets Arjuna of Indra. At his birth there is a prophecy that he will be a great warrior, acquire celestial weapons, and retrieve the fortunes of his family and race.

Pandu is still not satisfied. He wants more children and so asks Kunti to invoke some other god. Kunti, however, refuses saying that a woman having relationship with four men is said to be of loose morals while one with five is known as a harlot. Therefore, she firmly refuses to concede to any more of Pandu's requests. But would this rule apply to only men or also to relationships with the gods? Or were the gods only a euphemism for men? And if this was so, why did Kunti so insistently get Draupadi married to her five sons? As is seen later, politics and single-minded quest for power has more to do with it than morality or virtue.

After the birth of Kunti's sons, Maadri complains to Pandu that she too wants sons and wishes for Kunti to arrange for her as well. To rescue Maadri's grief of remaining childless Pandu requests Kunti, who readily yields and asks Maadri to think of the form of some celestial being from whom she would like to have a child. Reflecting a moment, Maadri thinks of the twin Ashvins who beget two sons upon her, the twins Nakula and Sahdeva, unrivalled on earth for their personal beauty. This enrages Kunti. On the one hand is Gandhari, her sister-in-law and hence a rival centre of power, producing a hundred sons, and on the other hand is Maadri, her co-wife, who gets two sons through only one invocation ringing danger bells. Kunti feels that Maadri has deceived her and given another opportunity, would surpass her in the number of sons she has. This is not acceptable. She firmly turns down any further requests and Pandu has no option but to accept Kunti's decision.

However, there is no end to Kunti's struggles. One day in spring, just as everything seems to be moving along smoothly, disaster strikes. Pandu accompanied by Maadri roams around in the woods where every branch is laden with new blossoms of spring. The air is seductive and Maadri is standing in a semi-transparent attire. Seeing the young and beautiful Maadri thus, the king's desire is kindled like a wild forest fire. Unable to control himself, he seizes her despite her protests and resistance. In the heat of the moment, he forgets the Rishi's curse. Pandu's reason, beguiled by the intoxication of his senses, leads to the end of his life.

Hearing Maadri's piteous weeping, as she clasps Pandu's senseless body, Kunti and the children rush to the spot. Extremely grieved and angry, Kunti reproaches Maadri pointing out that when she herself has been so careful all along, how could Maadri forget the curse and allow Pandu to approach her. No amount of Maadri's tearful protests satisfy her. Intermingled with Kunti's ire is perhaps deep-seated jealousy that Maadri experienced Pandu's love and saw in his face, a yearning for her, in the last moments of his life, a joy that Kunti could now could never experience. She wants to at least die with Pandu, but Maadri begs her to be allowed to follow him to the other world as she acknowledges that Kunti has greater strength and moral superiority. She accepts that she will never be able to look after Kunti's children and rear them as her own but Kunti, would be an equally willing and caring mother to Nakula and Sahdeva, as she would be to her three sons. Facing the guilt of having been the cause of Pandu's death she also realizes that now a long and intense struggle for the throne of Hastinapura is imminent if Pandu's children stake their claim to it. Maadri probably does not feel equal to dealing with that. With Kunti's permission, she self-immolates on Pandu's funeral pyre.

With Pandu's demise, the rishis ponder on the future course of action for Kunti and her sons, whom they regard their responsibility. They feel it is time to take them to Hastinapura and place them in the hands of Bhishma and Dhritarashtra. This move, of course, initiates the revival of hostilities as the Kauravas inevitably look upon their cousins to be eliminated as expeditiously as possible. Kunti has not only to remain watchful but also take care to never alienate the Kuru elders if the claim to the throne is to be realized.

At Hastinapura, the Pandavas are instructed together with the Kauravas by the two gurus — Dronacharya and Kripacharya. Arjuna is Drona's favourite. When they complete their education, and with Dhritarashtra's permission, Dronacharya organizes a tournament to enable the princes to demonstrate their proficiency. Just as the spectacular display of Arjuna's powers begins to mesmerize the people gathered around, a sound from the gate indicates the arrival of someone with tremendous strength and ability.

Everyone's eyes turn as Karna enters with his natural

golden mail and face brightened with gold earrings. He challenges Arjuna. Duryodhana is delighted. He embraces Karna and accepts him as an equal and a friend. Surya and Indra come out to watch the fight between their two sons but Kunti, recognizing Karna is instantly overwhelmed with the shock and trauma conflicting and confounding her mind. She is afraid as her two powerful sons clad in mail are ready to clash with each other. She also knows that she cannot prevent Karna's humiliation. Before the joust can begin, Kripacharya demands to know Karna's lineage and once that is known, it is very specifically announced that Karna is neither an equal in caste nor in status to participate at the event, which is only for royalty. Duryodhana immediately comes to Karna's rescue and declares him to be the king of Anga thereby cementing a lifelong friendship and ensuring Radheya's indebtedness and unswerving loyalty. Of course, Kunti is very happy to see her son Karna installed as the sovereign of Anga, but she chooses to be a silent witness to his success as well as to his ignominy.

The Pandavas grow from strength to strength, and this arouses the jealousy of the Kauravas. Things are tense in the Kuru court underneath the surface normalcy. The Pandavas are popular with the people and Dhritarashtra is forced to appoint Yudhishthira as the *Yuvaraja*, the heir apparent. This upsets Duryodhana immensely and rankles Dhritarashtra. The latter calls his counsellor Kanika seeking a solution to remedy the situation. Kanika advises that if the king wants his sons to succeed, he should get rid of the Pandavas and their mother.

With Dhritarashtra's passive consent Shakuni and Duryodhana plot a devious plan to burn Kunti and her sons in an inflammable house of lac, which Duryodhana gets constructed through his trusted counsellor, Purochana, at Varnavata, near the arsenal. Dhritarashtra persuades the Pandavas and Kunti to go there on the pretext that having become the *Yuvaraja*, Yudhishthira should now mingle with the people, and the festival in the honour of Shiva is a great opportunity. They are told that a special palace has been built for their stay. Yudhishthira senses an ulterior motive in Dhritarashtra's plan in sending him to Varnavata, as does Vidura. Other courtiers also suspect something, knowing that Dhritarashtra cannot bear the Pandavas' popularity and presence. Everyone wonders how Bhishma can permit them to go in the face of obvious danger. Vidura warns Yudhishthira of the perils that await them at Varnavata, and particularly in the house of lac.

Kunti wants to know the exact words of Vidura's warning as she prepares to take charge of the situation and save her sons from imminent death. While she had observed all previous attempts on the lives of her sons, during their childhood, she had remained a silent witness for fear of losing the support of the Kuru clan, but this present threat is too serious to be over-looked and she knows she must deal with it. At first, Kunti and the Pandavas debate whether they should occupy the house of lac at all, which is meant for their destruction. They conclude that they must not arouse suspicion in Dhritarashtra and the Kaurava brothers and indicate that they know anything, there-fore they must stay there and then formulate their plans of escape. Purochana insists on living with them, ostensibly to serve them, but, in reality, to keep a watch on them and to execute Duryodhana's plan at the appropriate time. His is lulled into complacency by seeing Kunti and the Pandavas cheerfully living in the house. He does not know that his own death is very near as the Pandavas finalize their strategies of escape.

Vidura sends a miner to secretly build a large subterranean passage that will enable the Pandavas to escape secretly when Purochana sets the house of lac on fire. On the appointed night, Kunti hosts a feast in which she feeds many Brahmins and other members of the populace. Among the guests are a Nishada woman who comes with her five sons; satiated with food and drinks, they are persuaded by Kunti to stay back for the night in the mansion. When all are asleep, including Purochana himself, Bhima sets fire to the house. It is assumed at that point of time that Purochana, who built the inflammable house and burnt it to eliminate Kunti and the Pandavas, got caught in it as well. The Pandavas and Kunti are thought to be dead as the unrecognizable charred bodies of the Nishada woman and her five sons are found in the debris. A secretly delighted Dhritarashtra performs their last rites with great display of apparent grief.

In the meantime, Kunti and the Pandavas escape through the subterranean passage to the forests where Vidura's trusted men meet them. They arrive on the banks of the River Ganga. On Vidura's instructions they are provided with a strong boat. Crossing the river, they proceed towards the south finding their way in the dark by starlight. Exhausted and thirsty, they suffer so much that Yudhishthira requests Bhima, who is the only one strong enough to do so, to carry them, together with their mother Kunti.

The Pandavas go from forest to forest. During their wanderings, they meet their grandfather Sage Veda Vyasa who leads them to the town of Ekachakra. Here they stay incognito in the house of a Brahmin, disguised as mendicants, to escape the clutches of Dhritarashtra and Duryodhana. Every night the Pandava brothers place before their mother what they collect by begging during the day and she divides the whole lot equally among them. Kunti is the cementing force between them as they all give her unswerving obedience. This is more than Gandhari can claim as Duryodhana repeatedly disobeys her.

One day, as the others are out begging, Bhima is alone with his mother. They hear loud and heart-rending wails coming from the Brahmin's house. Kunti, out of compassion and goodness, cannot remain indifferent to it. She tells Bhima that as

they are living in the Brahmin's house, they owe a debt of gratitude to him. A true person always repays more that he receives
by way of favours done to him; they are duty-bound to help the
Brahmin in whatever affliction has overtaken him. The
Brahmin explains that on the outskirts of the town lives a
rakshasa or demon named Vaka who is the self-acclaimed lord
of both the town and the country. He is a cannibal. Although he
protects the place well, in return he demands a human being
every day for his food together with a cartload of rice and two
buffaloes. Each family has been taking turns at sacrificing a
member of its household and now it is his family's turn.

On hearing this, Kunti says that the Brahmin has only one
son while she herself has five sons and so she voluntarily
decides to send one of her sons. The Brahmin agrees very
reluctantly and Bhima pledges that he will not only go but also
rid the town of such a cruel lord. Yudhishthira is very
displeased with his mother and, although it is very uncharac-
teristic of him, he forcefully expresses his disagreement. It is
folly, to endanger Bhima, the strongest of them all and on
whom they all depend on a great deal, not only for their day-to-
day safety but also for their victory over the Kauravas. The only
other time that he openly expresses his strong disapproval of
her actions is at the end of the war, when Kunti reveals that
Karna was his elder brother, her first born.

Kunti's answer to her son proves to be a brilliant lesson in
statecraft. The Pandava's sojourn in the forests and the cohabi-
tation with commoners is the ideal education on governance
and kingship for them as they imbibe first-hand knowledge of
how the common people live. Kunti says, having enjoyed the
hospitality of the Brahmin, it is their duty to repay it. A Kshatriya who helps a Brahmin acquires great merit. Besides, she is
confident that Bhima will defeat and kill the asura and return
unharmed. In any case, a king must protect even the meanest of
his subjects who seeks him out. If he fulfils his responsibility,

even in his next birth he will be in the royal line and will also command prosperity together with the respect of other kings. Sage Vyasa himself had told Kunti this. Thus, what she is really saying is that if Yudhishthira aspires to be the king, he must conduct himself as one. He should never be indebted to his subjects, and always give them confidence in his power and ability to protect them. Only then can he hope to be prosperous and enjoy the respect of others who are his equals. This, he must never forget, whatever be their condition and here, in any case, the risk is minimal given Bhima's phenomenal strength and ability. He has already demonstrated his power on many earlier occasions including defeating the powerful cannibalistic forest demon, King Hidimba and saving their lives. Even then, Kunti demonstrates her sure grasp of statecraft. After Bhima defeats Hidimba, she encourages him to marry the demon's sister, Hidimbi, thus entering a liaison with the forest people. Later, Ghatotkacha, Bhima's son from the alliance, fights valiantly for the Pandavas at the war.

As Kunti anticipates, Bhima slays the asura and the Pandavas continue to live peacefully till another learned Brahmin comes with the news of the forthcoming *swayamvara* of the beautiful Draupadi, the daughter of King Drupada of Panchala. The Pandavas grow restless on hearing this. Kunti immediately understands their state of mind and proposes that they all go to Panchala; Veda Vyasa, their grandfather, has already prophesied during a visit at the Brahmin's house that Draupadi will be their common wife.

The Pandavas go to Panchala where they stay with a potter, another commoner and even lower in the social hierarchy than the poor Brahmin with whom they are living at Ekachakra. Great preparations are on in Panchala and there is tremendous excitement about Draupadi's *swayamvara*. The brothers meet Veda Vyasa there who commands them to proceed to Drupada's abode for the occasion. They go disguised as Brahmin youth. Great kings have assembled to try their luck at winning Draupadi's hand. Her brother, Dhrishtadyumna, informs them of the difficult condition of marksmanship with bow and arrow that must be fulfilled. When all the assembled kings and princes fail, Karna rises and strings the bow; the first one to achieve that feat so far; but before he can shoot the target of the eye of the fish rotating on the ceiling, Draupadi boldly denounces his claim and says she that will not accept a *suta-putra* (the son of a low caste) as her husband.

Laughing in vexation and glancing at the Sun, Karna sits down, throwing his bow aside. Then comes Arjuna, in a Brahmin's garb, amid much speculation and trepidation in the assembly. He strings the bow and with ease fulfils the specified and extremely challenging condition. The unsuccessful monarchs exclaim in frustration, anger mingled with grief, and despair, while a clamour of wonder and excitement arises from the others in the assembly. Drupada is overjoyed but simultaneously prepares his forces to thwart the onslaught of the defeated kings on himself and on the Brahmin youth, in case the situation arises.

Amidst the din and clamour, Yudhishthira and the twins, Nakula and Sahdeva, slip out and return home to Kunti. Confident that Arjuna and Bhima can ably defend themselves should the need arise, they undoubtedly want to inform Kunti of all that has happened at Drupada's court. She knows where they had gone. The assembled kings rush at the disguised Arjuna and at Drupada. Bhima and Arjuna easily hold them at bay. Watching them, Sri Krishna, who is present there together with his brother Balarama, points out to the latter that his aunt and cousins obviously did not perish at Varnavata and that these two valiant 'brahmins' are none other than Arjuna and Bhima. This means that Arjuna himself, and not an ordinary brahmin youth, has won the fair Draupadi's hand. This had been Drupada's secret desire too. Kunti, meanwhile, is anxiously waiting for Bhima and Arjuna to return. As her sons get delayed, she wonders whether Sage Vyasa himself has predicted incorrectly. It follows, therefore, that Kunti is under no misconception that her sons are out for their daily round of begging as mendicants. She knows they are at Draupadi's *swayamvara* and before Bhima and Arjuna return she also knows of the events that have occurred at the court.

When Arjuna and Bhima do come back and standing at the door, call out to their mother that they have brought their daily alms, Kunti is aware of what she is saying, when she declares, "Share whatever you have procured equally among yourselves." It has been commonly assumed that Kunti, without seeing Draupadi, asks them to share what they have got and that the moment she sees Draupadi she realizes the implications of what she has inadvertently said. This does not seem to add up when the sequence of events is put together. Her answer is obviously a calculated move. Kunti wants an unbreakable alliance with the kingdom of Panchala. She is aware that Drupada is already smarting from the humiliation of half his kingdom being taken away by Drona with Arjuna's help, which the guru asked his student to procure for him in lieu of *guru-dakshina*. Arjuna won this by the force of his arms from Drupada for Dronacharya. Therefore, Drupada may, in fact, want Arjuna as a groom for Draupadi — to have such a great warrior by his side rather than standing opposite to him, if he ever wants to retrieve his kingdom. After all, he had prayed for a son and got Dhrishtadyumna only to take revenge on Drona. Kunti also knows that she is the single uniting force among the brothers and that she alone can keep their sight fixed on the throne of Hastinapura. As she advances in age, she can only be replaced by one strong woman rather than by five, someone who has the great capacity to hold them together. Who better than Draupadi? Future events prove her right.

Having made the declaration, Kunti then turns to

Yudhishthira to find a way out of the dilemma; once again, fully aware of what she is doing because he is the most knowledgeable in the law of dharma and he alone can find a solution in conformity with it, which is also suitable to her. Yudhishthira finally decides that Draupadi will be the common wife of all of them, and together with Sage Vyasa, convinces Drupada that this is in conformity with dharma. It is significant that throughout the discussion between Sage Vyasa and King Drupada on whether Draupadi could lawfully marry the five brothers, Kunti keeps the discussion on the desired channel by insisting that her words cannot go in vain. She says that not only is the act virtuous, as both Yudhishthira and Sage Vyasa have said so, but that it is also in accordance with the prophesied future.

After the marriage, Kunti gradually hands over the reins to Draupadi. That is why when the Pandavas go to the forest on losing the game of dice, Kunti does not accompany them. Draupadi now starts performing the functions that Kunti has done previously, of keeping them focused on winning the throne of Hastinapura. Although Kunti is terribly afflicted by the disastrous turn of events after the game of dice, she consoles Draupadi and asks her not to grieve over the calamities that have overtaken them. Since Draupadi is both virtuous and wise, she, Kunti, has no need to instruct her on her duties towards her husbands. She, however, feels bound to remind Draupadi that good women never allow their heart to be overwhelmed by what is inevitable. Kunti chooses to stay back in the midst the hostility at Hastinapura, although at Vidura's home and not at the palace. She wants her presence to be a constant reminder of the injustice done to her sons and of their claim to the throne.

That she is a centre of power in Hastinapura is borne out by the fact that when Sri Krishna comes on his last peace mission to the Kauravas, he first goes to meet his aunt Kunti, after meeting Vidura. She uses two powerful emotional weapons to ensure Sri Krishna's sympathy — her personal plight at the exile of her sons and the unacceptable humiliation of her daughter-in-law, Draupadi. She laments that her sons are suffering great hardships in the forest; that her grief for them far surpasses all the loss of wealth and the hostility that they faced at the Kaurava court. For herself, she reiterates that life has always been full of struggle. Given away like a toy by her father to Kuntibhoja in her childhood; abandoned by both her father Surasena and foster father Kuntibhoja, as neither ever came to her aid; and since then, Dhritarashtra, whom she has regarded as her father-in-law, has shown nothing but animosity towards her. While she says all this to draw the sympathetic compassion of her nephew Sri Krishna before he goes in for the negotiations, there is a lot of truth in it.

She then talks of Draupadi, who she says is dearer to her than even her sons. Draupadi like her, she laments, has not seen her children for fourteen years. She can never forgive the Kauravas for dragging Draupadi into the Kaurava court and being openly humiliated and molested by her own brothers-in-law. It also is very painful that the brave Pandavas warriors spent the past year of the exile in concealment. Kunti is sure that righteousness and truth are on their side and therefore the Pandavas will overcome their sorrows. She recalls the prophecy at the time of Arjuna's birth that he will conquer the whole world and that his fame will reach the heavens. If dharma is not a myth, she asserts, this must certainly happen.

Sri Krishna consoles Kunti by assuring her that there is no one in the world like her. Daughter of Surasena, she was, by marriage admitted into the Ajamida's race. High born and married with dignity into a royal family, she is like a lotus transplanted from one mighty lake into another. Adored by her husband, the wife of a hero, she is the mother of heroic sons. Not only the Pandavas, but he himself salutes her, says Sri Krishna. Thus, consoled by Sri Krishna, she advises him to do whatever he thinks is proper without sacrificing righteousness. After taking her counsel, Sri Krishna proceeds to Duryodhana's mansion.

The negotiations fail; before leaving Hastinapura, Sri Krishna comes back to Kunti to briefly narrate all that transpired in the assembly of Kurus. Kunti now sends a poignant message for each one of her sons as she is convinced that they have no option but to fight. To Yudhishthira her message is that his virtue is decreasing because of his inaction. Much as he may be attracted to the ascetic life of the forest, he must act according to the duties of his order. The Kshatriya, she said, was created for war and to protect his people with the prowess of his arms. There is the example of the royal sage Muchukunda who refused the gift of sovereignty over the earth because he said that he would only enjoy the rule over what he had won by his own endeavours. Further, says Kunti, Yudhishthira must never forget the duties of a king. He should remember that while the sixth part of all virtue practiced by subjects accrues to the king, the virtue that the king himself practices confers godhead upon him. However, if he perpetrates sin, he goes to *naraka* (hell). All orders of society must adhere to their respective duties, and it is for the king to ensure this. Thus, the king ushers in the age or the yuga by his actions and is not to consider himself subordinate to Time. A king cannot blame Time for his misfortunes or those of the state. If he enables the Krita or the Sat Yuga or Age to set in, he enjoys heaven and more; with the Treta Yuga, he can only partly savour heaven; with the Dwapara Yuga, he just about manages to get his dues. But the one who allows the Kali Yuga to set in, suffers hell. A weak-hearted king never obtains merit. Kunti makes it clear that she disapproves of Yudhishthira's point of view and urges him to do his kingly duties. He must fight like a king and not let down the name of his ancestors. Kunti further tries to boost Yudhishthira's morale by reminding him of the stirring story of Vidula, a high-born woman of great foresight who rebukes her son for sinking into depression after being defeated by the king of Sindhus. She exhorts him to avenge his defeat concluding that only a man who acquires greatness through his personal exertions can succeed in winning fame in this world and a blessed state in the next. Kunti knows that it is most vital to arouse Yudhishthira who is of a forgiving nature to a fault and abhors war or any form of conflict.

To Bhima, Kunti says that the time has come for which Kshatriya women bear sons and that he must live up to his fame in the ensuing battle. She reminds Arjuna of the great prophesies that resounded at the time of his birth predicting that he will vanquish the Kurus in battle. Aided by Bhima he will conquer the whole earth and his fame will reach the very heavens. She urges him to now make the prophecy come true. She emphasizes that he cannot ignore Draupadi's humiliation and urges him that at any moment of doubt to follow the path pointed out by Draupadi, rather than by Yudhishthira. She reminds Nakula and Sahdeva that they should only covet those enjoyments that are acquired by their prowess more than life itself. She impresses upon all of them that the insult to Draupadi cannot be overlooked and must be avenged. In her message for Draupadi, she urges her to stay on the path of virtue and do all that is becoming of her. The connotations of the message are obvious. Her messages are according to her accurate reading of her sons. While she is not sure about Yudhishthira, she has no doubt that Draupadi will be insistent that the war must be fought.

Sri Krishna carefully listens to what Kunti has to say and then departs, taking leave of the Kuru warriors with Bhishma at their head. The import of all the factors that have come into play at this juncture, and the determined messages that Kunti sends to her sons and daughter-in-law are not lost on the Kaurava elders. They are convinced that the Pandavas will follow their mother's directives and the consequence will be the certain defeat of the Kauravas. They try to dissuade Duryodhana from war. They warn him that Draupadi's humiliation cannot be refuted. The strength of the two sides has also been tested on several occasions in the past and the Pandavas have always succeeded in getting the better of the Kaurava warriors. They strongly counsel peace but their efforts are of no avail in front of Duryodhana's stubborn determination to fight.

Vidura is extremely dejected on the failure of Sri Krishna's peace mission. He now sees no way of avoiding the battle and the consequent destruction. As he talks with Kunti about it, she too realizes that eventually it will only be a Pyrrhic victory. There is now only one way that the carnage can be prevented and that is to reveal to Karna the truth of his birth, as a lot depends upon this. Karna is, after all, a key warrior on the Kaurava side, one on whom Duryodhana depends completely. It seems worth a try and so she decides to swallow her pride and go to him that very day. When Karna is praying on the bank of the River Ganga with his face towards the sun, Kunti reaches there and waits quietly for him to finish his worship. As he turns and sees her, he greets her with great respect. Kunti now tells him that he is her son and reminds him of what is her due from him as his mother. Yudhishthira's prosperity, acquired through Arjuna's bravery, has been wrested from the Pandavas by the crooked stratagems of the Kauravas. Snatching it back from the sons of Dhritarashtra, Kunti urges him to enjoy it, as her first born. Kunti does not even mention here the insult to Draupadi and Karna's role in that because situational expediency demands that she wins over Karna. Surya himself corroborates Kunti's story and urges his son to follow his mother's advice, but Karna does not waver. He recounts his life-long anguish and humiliation due to discrimination because of being seen as a low-caste charioteer's son, only because his mother abandoned him at birth and never acknowledged him thereafter. However, he promises Kunti that apart from Arjuna he will not slay any of the other Pandava brothers. But if he succeeds in killing Arjuna in battle he will achieve great merit; on being slain by him, he will die covered in glory. To Kunti, he promises, with great irony, that regardless of whether it is himself or Arjuna who dies in battle, she will as always, be known as the mother of five sons. Kunti has no option but to be satisfied with this. While she has succeeded in securing the life of four of her sons, she has at the same time handicapped Karna because while the Pandavas, not knowing the truth, will leave no stone unturned to defeat and kill him, he will be bound by his word to Kunti. That is exactly what happens on several occasions as he lets the other Pandavas off even when he has them in positions of obvious disadvantage.

At the end of the war, Kunti visits the battlefield. Dhritarashtra asks Yudhishthira to arrange for the funerals of the dead warriors with all the honours due to them. In a sudden paroxysm of grief, and to ensure that Yudhishthira accords appropriate honours to the departed Karna, Kunti cannot control herself and reveals to Yudhishthira that Karna, the great warrior slain by Arjuna in the battle, is in fact their elder brother. She explains that he was her premarital son born from Surya, but she never found the courage to reveal this truth earlier. Yudhishthira is beside himself with utmost grief on hearing this. He feels more weighed down with despair for Karna than he is even for Abhimanyu or for the sons of Draupadi. He harshly upbraids his mother and pronounces the curse that henceforth women will never be able to keep any secrets.

Once Yudhishthira ascends the throne, Kunti gradually fades away from public visibility. Having accomplished her mission, she has no desire to interfere either with the affairs of the state or with her daughter-in-law. Several years later with the kingdom settled down, Dhritarashtra and Gandhari prepare for their final departure to the forests. Kunti decides to accompany them. Yudhishthira and each one of her other sons together with Draupadi try to persuade her to stay and finally, after a lifetime of struggles, enjoy the royal status of the queen mother, but she is adamant. Having fulfilled what she set out to do, Kunti now wants to live the last phase of her life with dignity instead of getting embroiled either in the affairs of the family or of the State. She has learnt enough from life's experiences to know what to expect from families and what the expediencies of statecraft are. She knows that her stature will be reduced if she now asserts herself before her daughter-in-law and that her influence will diminish on its own.

In a magnificent speech, Kunti explains her position. She recalls instilling courage in her sons when they were cheerless. She constantly inspired them so that never again would they have to suffer the ignominy of going into the forests and living in misery. She ensured that Bhima, possessed of great strength and prowess, did not sink into insignificance and ruin; that Arjuna did not remain despondent; and that Nakula and Sahdeva, who always look up to their elder brothers, were not weakened. She motivated them and confirmed that Draupadi would never again have to endure the kind of wrongs that had been inflicted upon her, and her violated honour was not left unavenged. She says that if she had not instilled courage in them through the story of Vidula and her sons, the race of Pandu would have been lost or disgraced. The sons and grandsons of a person who bring a race to infamy never attain the regions of the righteous. Whatever she ever did was for them and now she has no desires left for herself. In any case, she does not wish to enjoy the sovereignty won by her sons. By the merit of her own penances, she wants to now re-join her husband in the regions of felicity to which he has gone.

Hearing her words, the Pandavas no longer urge Kunti to stay. Dhritarashtra tries, through Gandhari, to dissuade Kunti, but the latter's decision is firm. In Kunti's absence the Pandavas become extremely cheerless, while she spends her time in the forests doing severe ascetic penances and serving Gandhari and Dhritarashtra. After some time, Yudhishthira, accompanied by Draupadi, his brothers, their wives, and the other Kuru ladies, visits Kunti, Gandhari, and Dhritarashtra in the forest. Sage Vyasa reaches there at the same time. Kunti asks him where had she sinned; was it by abandoning Karna, and then by not disclosing his identity at the appropriate time? When Sage Vyasa reassures her that she was not sinful she expresses the desire to see Karna once more. Sage Vyasa promises that all those who are present there that very night, will see the deceased warriors, their loved ones, as they are all in heaven. That will ease everyone's pain and bring a closure to their grief. The night of union is of great satisfaction to all. Thereafter, Dhritarashtra resolves to leave his body and together with Gandhari and Kunti they perish in a forest fire.

4

DRAUPADI

If the throne of Hastinapura was the prize, Draupadi was the pivot on which the war of the *Mahabharata* turned. Among all the queens of Hastinapura, she is the only one who successfully interrogates the patriarchal norms, openly challenges the men and asserts herself as their equal. On many occasions she sustains and protects her five husbands instead of it being the other way round. In fact, they, especially Yudhishthira, let her down at the most crucial and humiliating moments — her disrobing in the Kuru court, Jayadratha's attempt to abduct her, and Kichaka's offensive assault at Virata's court. Despite all the humiliation heaped on her, the five warriors, the Pandavas, at some stage or the other, seek peace rather than revenge. Even during the final journey over the Himalaya, when Draupadi falls first, not one of them stops to help her. Yet she rises like a Phoenix, above all adversity, to carve an inerasable niche for herself in the narrative.

Her strength and courage have contributed to her independent status as a cult figure. She is worshipped as a goddess throughout the country, either directly or indirectly. In South India, the cult of Draupadi is extremely powerful. Temples devoted to her stand even today, where she is worshipped in her own right. Despite being the wife of five husbands, and the mother of five sons, she is worshipped in South India as a virgin goddess who purifies her devotees of their sins and brings salvation. The worship of Draupadi is found throughout Tamil Nadu and beyond. The centre of the Draupadi cult has been identified at Gingee in South Arcot, Tamil Nadu. Gingee's Draupadi temple is recognized as the primal shrine of the goddess. Some other new temples use a Gingee stone for their image or the Gingee soil on which to install the image. Her worship was also carried overseas, to places far and wide, like Sri Lanka, Singapore, Fiji, and Reunion Island, by the people of South India as they crossed the seas in search of employment driven by harsh economic conditions in their homeland. Almost every sugar plantation owned by the people of Indian origin in Reunion Island has a temple where Draupadi is the primary deity. Sometimes, she is accompanied by Arjuna; often by Mariamma, another village goddess; and occasionally by her mother-in-law, Kunti.

CELEBRATED AND WORSHIPPED

There are festivals devoted to Draupadi, which include performances in three different modes: *Parata Pricankam* or the recitation of the epic in Tamil by high-caste professional singers; *Terukuittu*, or street drama although it is performed on a stage by itinerant all-male troupers, the performers belonging to the so-called 'lower' castes; and the local enactments of episodes from the *Mahabharata*, adding richness and variety to the epic itself. Her devotees, who usually belong to the lower strata in the social hierarchical scale, see her as the protector of the downtrodden and the oppressed. Draupadi is the protector goddess of the lower echelons in the societal hierarchy; a village and folk deity providing succour and safety; the Devi of the forest people, rising above the confining patriarchal norms; ever pure in spite of her five husbands; and ever renewed. She is an affirmation of human freedom and courage in the face of adversity that makes a person rise above all trials and emerge the winner.

By their performances, the participants identify with the Pandavas and express their devotion to Draupadi. Born from the sacrificial fire, Draupadi purifies herself in myths through fire before moving from one brother to the other. Her devotees also emulate her in the fire-walking rituals as they walk on a bed of hot coals. It is commonly understood to be the Pandava army successfully following Draupadi and the Pandavas across the fires of the Kurukshetra battle. In Sri Lanka, it also symbolizes the ritual of animal sacrifice to the goddess, the fire-walking devotee being ready to the offer himself to Draupadi.

Two interesting guardian images can be seen in all her temples that deviate from the classical epic traditions. One image is of Muttal Ravuttan, a Muslim cavalry trooper who is devoted to her. This may reflect the impact of Islam on Draupadi worship in its formative period. He is not only her devotee but also protects her, neutralizing impurity and extreme forms of sacrificial violence. The second image is of Pottu Raja, the Buffalo King, whose source is Mahishasura, the Buffalo Demon slain by Kali. Here he carries weapons that, in the hands of the goddess, transformed him into a devotee. In the myth associated with the Draupadi cult, Pottu Raja leads the Pandava army. Draupadi has been linked to the other goddesses worshipped throughout India, revealing layers of parallels and similarities to demonstrate a pan-India culture of the worship of the goddess and thereby of Shakti — strength, courage, endurance, the power to annihilate when required and emerge triumphant in life-affirming creation that brings continuous hope and faith for future generations.

·   ·   ·

Born with a purpose

Draupadi, like Satyavati, had an unusual birth. Drupada had lost half his kingdom to Dronacharya, who to avenge himself of a past insult had demanded it as *gurudakshina* from Arjuna. Distressed, Drupada wandered to many ashramas of Brahmins searching those who were well skilled in sacrificial rites. He came to the ashrama of two great sages Yaja and Upayaja. He told Upayaja that he desired a son who could slay Drona. At first, Upayaja did not agree but after being persuaded for a year, he said that while he himself would not perform the required sacrificial rites, as it was against his principles, his brother Yaja did not have any such scruples. Drupada then requested Yaja to perform rites by which he could obtain a son who would slay Drona. Yaja not only agreed but also persuaded Upayaja to assist him. From the sacrificial fire appeared a son and a daughter. First arose the son whose body was encased in an armour, and he wore a crown on his head. In his one hand, he carried a sword and in the other bow and arrows. Hence, he was called Dhrishtadyumna. It was prophesied at his birth that he would destroy Drona. After him a daughter emerged; she was called Panchali, was exceedingly beautiful with her dark flowing tresses and her body fragrant with the scent of blue lotuses. Being dark in complexion she was also known as Krishna.

At her birth an incorporeal voice said that she would be the greatest of all women and the cause of the destruction of many Kshatriyas. Seeking nothing for herself, she would embody the divine will destroying a decadent age in which ethics or dharma had been reduced to expediency, narrow self-interest, and hypocrisy. The birth of a new age had to be ushered in. It had happened once before when sage Parashurama had exterminated the Kshatriyas and a new order had been brought forth by the union of the Kshatriyas and the Brahmins, a combination of valour and wisdom.

Draupadi's polyandrous marriage is well known. Two explanations are given for this in the text itself. Sage Vyasa tells the Pandavas of the legend of an illustrious rishi with a beautiful and accomplished daughter, who does not get a suitable husband. Therefore, she begins severe ascetic penances and soon gratifies Lord Shiva who promises to grant her any boon that she desires. She asks for a husband, but Mahadeva says that she would have five husbands in another life because in her impatience she repeated her desire five times. That girl, he said, has now been born as Draupadi and is destined to be the wife of them all. He then tells them to go to the capital of Panchalas and win her. The second explanation is that Shiva is playing with Parvati when he is rudely interrupted by Indra, who arrogantly introduces himself as the Lord of the world. For this, he is penalized, split into five, and sent to the earth as the five Pandavas. Sri, Indra's consort, follows as Draupadi and so although she marries the five brothers, they are in essence one. Hence, in one story it is Shiva's boon and in the other his wrath, but the conclusion is the same. Since Draupadi is Sri, the symbol of beauty and prosperity, by losing her, the Pandavas lose all their 'Sri', which can only restore when she is avenged.

Polyandry, in any case, seems to have been at one time, an accepted custom and practice. Yudhishthira, in his attempts to convince Drupada, narrates the story of the Rishi Utathya and his wife Mamata, narrated by Bhishma to Satyavati in another context. Mamata is already pregnant from Utathya, and their child has heard and memorized the Vedas while in her womb, foreshadowing Abhimanyu's learning the techniques of the Chakravyuha in Subhadra's womb. Vrihaspati, her husband's younger brother, approaches her. Although Mamata tells him of her condition, he cannot resist her beauty and unites with her. When the child in the womb protests that he has already occupied the space within and that there was no room for another, Vrihaspati curses him with blindness as he had been interrupted while enjoying the pleasure commonly due to all living beings. Hence, the child Dirghatamas, is born blind. The episode parallels the later disabling of Pandu, which prevents him from cohabiting with his wives because of his interrupting the mating of deer.

In his attempt to convince Drupada that his daughter could rightly marry all the five brothers, Sage Vyasa refers to the authority of the Puranas in which the virtuous Jatila married seven rishis simultaneously. Also, an ascetic's daughter born of a tree united herself with ten brothers, called the Prachetas. Sage Vyasa's stories may just have been attempts to rationalize the polyandrous marriage in the light of the imposition of an increasingly narrow sexual code according to patriarchal norms. Therefore, Yudhishthira concludes that since the marriage is acceptable as dharma, Draupadi should agree to his suggestion to marry all the five brothers.

It is curious that Draupadi should remain silent when such a vital issue pertaining to her life is being discussed. She is not one to remain quiet and never does, neither before nor after. After all, at her own *swayamvara*, she boldly stands in the assembly of warriors, princes, and kings, to firmly state that Karna, whatever may be his valour and skills, is not acceptable as a husband, thus overriding the condition put forth by her father to assert her choice. What can explain her silence? One reason offered is that she may have been Drupada's daughter from a woman other than his wife, or alternately a product of levirate relationship and so, does not feel confident enough to speak. The description of the extraordinary birth as an adult through the sacrificial fire may only be an attempt to gloss over these possibilities. But given her past behaviour, Draupadi's silence can only mean that she consents since the marriage is sanctified by dharma.

Arjuna's winning Draupadi's hand comes as a rude shock to Duryodhana and Duhshasana. It means two things: Firstly, the scheme to destroy the Pandavas in the house of lac failed. Secondly, not only are the Pandavas alive but now, allied with Drupada and Dhrishtadyumna, they are even more powerful and formidable than before. Duryodhana, accompanied by his brothers, his uncle Shakuni, Ashwatthama, Karna, and Kripacharya, returns to his capital with a heavy heart. Vidura is overjoyed to hear that the Pandavas have won Draupadi's hand, and excitedly tells Dhritarashtra that his son has obtained her hand in marriage. At first, Dhritarashtra is delighted thinking that his eldest son Duryodhana has won Draupadi but when he realizes that it is the Pandavas, his joy turns to immense resentment and anxiety, although he keeps up appearances before Vidura. Something needs to be done to prevent the Pandavas from getting too powerful. Dhritarashtra, then, takes counsel with Vidura, Karna, Drona, Bhishma and others on the future course of action now that it has been revealed that the Pandavas are alive and have married Draupadi. Going by a consensual decision, Dhritarashtra invites the Pandavas together with Draupadi and Kunti back to the kingdom and asks Vidura to carry his message to them. On reaching Panchala, Vidura enquires after the welfare of the Pandavas and seeks Drupada's permission to take the brothers to Hastinapura together with Draupadi and Kunti. Drupada expresses joy at being allied to Hastinapura but says the decision of going there rests with the Pandavas. Yudhishthira agrees to go and with Drupada's consent they head to Hastinapura where they are received with great pomp and honour.

To settle the issue of succession the kingdom is divided and the Pandavas are given Khandavaprastha to reside in separately, so that no dispute should arise between them and their cousins. Accepting this decision, Yudhishthira, along with his brothers, Kunti, and Draupadi moves to Khandavaprastha. With the help of Veda Vyasa, they mark out a sacred and auspicious region for their city. With Sri Krishna's help the barren land is transformed into a very beautiful and prosperous kingdom.

As the Pandavas settle down, Sri Krishna returns to Dwarka together with Balarama. After a while, the sage Narada visits the Pandavas and advises Yudhishthira to work out a system of sharing Draupadi equally between them as otherwise it can cause dissension. He narrates the story of the two asura brothers, Sunda and Upasunda, grandsons of the great asura, Hiranyakashipu. Always united, they performed severe ascetic penances together in the mountains of the Vindhyas and finally, obtained several boons from Brahma, such as, the knowledge of all weapons and of all powers of illusion, great strength and the ability to assume any form at will. The only thing that Brahma did not grant them was immortality because their primary aim was sovereignty over the three worlds. Having obtained these boons, the brothers began on their journey of conquests and laid numerable towns and cities desolate with ruthless slaughter. Perturbed by all the happenings, all the celestials and the great rishis went to Brahma for help and asked him to create a young woman capable of captivating the brothers with the aim of creating dissent. Brahma created the beautiful Tilottama, who was asked to go and charm the two brothers. Eventually, maddened by their passion for her, the two brothers killed each other. Therefore, warns Narada, the Pandavas should establish some rules among themselves, regarding their common wife Draupadi, so that there is no discord. Accordingly, it is decided that when any one of them is with Draupadi, none of the other four must enter that room and the one who does must retire into the forest for twelve years, passing his days as a celibate.

The Pandavas continue to reside at Khandavaprastha and bring many kings under their sway. Draupadi loves all the five Pandavas and takes great a delight in them as they do in her. After some time, it so happens that some robbers lift the cattle of a Brahmin. Filled with anger the Brahmin comes to the palace in Khandavaprastha, reproving the Pandavas. He demands that they pursue the robbers immediately and restore his cattle to him. Arjuna promises that he will go immediately after the dacoits as otherwise he would be failing in his duty and the blame will attach to the king for not providing timely protecting to his subjects. It so happens that the chamber where the weapons are kept is occupied by Yudhishthira and Draupadi. Arjuna is caught in a dilemma. He cannot enter the chamber without prior permission; and cannot follow the dacoits without his weapons. He finally decides that it is more important to aid the Brahmin even if it means being banished to the forests for twelve years.

Having decided this course of action, Arjuna enters the private chamber, and with Yudhishthira's permission, takes the weapons to go with the Brahmin. After he restores the Brahmin's cattle to him, he returns and begs Yudhishthira's leave to go to the woods according to the rule established between them. Yudhishthira is filled with grief and tries to dissuade him from going but Arjuna is determined. Finally with the king's permission, Arjuna prepares for life in the forests. Perhaps, Arjuna loves Draupadi too much to share her with anyone else, and since destiny has taken the course that it has, he chooses to create an excuse to go far away from her and build a life of his own. He, of course, does not keep his vow of celibacy and enters several matrimonial alliances.

The Pandavas continue to prosper and eventually decide to hold the Rajasuya Yagna that will give them imperial sway over all other kings. This has obvious potential for strife, which does happen, resulting in the beheading of Shishupala, the king of Chedi; but more importantly, this fuels the fire of jealousy and hatred in Duryodhana and the Kauravas. After all, Yudhishthira is the junior partner in the kingdom and belongs to the junior branch of the family. Dhritarashtra is the elder and the ruler. The Rajasuya Yagna can be construed as rather presumptuous of Yudhishthira and an open challenge to the authority of Dhritarashtra, Duryodhana, and the Kaurava clan.

Duryodhana arrives in Khandavaprastha accompanied by Shakuni and others. Yudhishthira's palace is exquisite with fascinating illusions created by Mayasura. At one point, Duryodhana mistakes a crystal surface for a pool of water and draws up his clothes. At another time, he falls into a lake of water, filled with lotuses, that he believes to be a crystal surface, due to the earlier illusion. He blunders through other such illusions like banging his head against a closed crystal door thinking it to be open space. At this point, in one version, Bhima and some servants laugh at and mock Duryodhana, but in another version it is said that Draupadi jeers at him, saying that a blind man's son can only be blind. This fills him with wrath. Perhaps that is why he is so harsh with Draupadi later when Yudhishthira loses the game of dice. He cannot bear to have been scorned by her. He has not only lost Draupadi to the Pandavas, but now she is making fun of him at a time when the Pandavas are threatening to get more powerful and prosperous than him. This is too much for him to take, so he tells Shakuni that he will destroy himself unless something is done to prevent the Pandavas from gaining imperial sway over the world together with the prosperity that will come with it. Shakuni explains that the Pandavas, with their allies, are invincible in war but that he will find another way to defeat them. He knows that Yudhishthira has a weakness for the game of dice and he, Shakuni, has the knack to load the dice to defeat the opponent. They can use the stratagem of inviting Yudhishthira to the game and win the kingdom for Duryodhana that cannot be won through a fair war.

The game of dice and Draupadi's humiliation

Duryodhana persuades Dhritarashtra and, despite Vidura's advice and warning, the game of dice is arranged between the Kauravas and the Pandavas. Shakuni playing for the former and Yudhishthira for the latter. In this game Yudhishthira loses his kingdom, his entire wealth, his brothers and even himself and then he stakes Draupadi. Shakuni 'wins' her for Duryodhana, who then commands that Draupadi be brought into the court. She is now their slave to do whatever they like with her. She will be forced to stay with the rest of the serving women and sweep their chambers. Vidura warns Duryodhana and the Kauravas not to cheat the Pandavas of their wealth as this act will later become the cause of their destruction. However, Duryodhana orders that Draupadi be brought to the court. Dhritarashtra, sitting on the throne with the right to say the last word, does not contradict his son. He reviles Vidura as one who has never wished the Kauravas any prosperity and is now raving in fear. First the servant of the court fearfully goes to fetch Draupadi and tells her of all that has happened. Draupadi is shocked and appalled but gathering herself together she commands the servant to go and enquire of Yudhishthira whom he lost first, her or himself. She orders him to ascertain this and return to her. This is a bold and courageous challenge to the entire Kuru clan, to their patriarchal norms, and their hollow moral values.

The messenger poses Draupadi's question to the court. While Yudhishthira sits in humiliated and ashamed silence, Duryodhana orders that Draupadi should come there and ask the question herself; the messenger once again goes to Draupadi to convey the message. In his opinion, the weak-brained King Yudhishthira will not be able to protect her. Draupadi, however, adamantly sends him back once again with her question. The messenger repeats the question at the court, but the Pandavas speak not a word, as they sit hanging their heads in abject defeat. Yudhishthira, in the meantime, sends a trusted messenger to Draupadi saying that although she is in her season with only one cloth over her body, she should come to the court as the Pandavas are bound by their promise and are at a loss as to what they can do to protect her. Duryodhana, gladdened at the humiliation of the Pandavas, once again instructs the messenger to bring Draupadi to the court. The *suta*, terrified of Draupadi's wrath, asks what he should say to her this time. This irritates Duryodhana so much that he orders his brother Duhshasana to go instead and forcibly drag her to the court. Eager to avenge the insults heaped upon him at Yudhishthira's Rajasuya Yagna and to settle the scores of his over-consuming jealousy, he swaggers around saying that his enemies are now his slaves and helpless. Duhshasana informs Draupadi that she has no choice but to present herself in the court as she has been won by the Kauravas. Hearing this, Draupadi rises in great fear and affliction, rubs her pale face, and runs to the place where the ladies of Dhritarashtra's household sit. This enrages Duhshasana. Seizing her by her hair, he drags her to the assembly hall. Her body bent, Draupadi faintly cries that not only is she a daughter-in-law of this king, she is in her season and is clad in but one cloth, and that he is going beyond the bounds of decency to force her thus to the assembly. But Duhshasana cruelly retorts that he does not really care about her condition. She has been won at the game of dice, made their slave, and hence she has now to live among their serving women.

With dishevelled hair and half her attire loosened, dragged by Duhshasana, Draupadi is consumed with anger, but faintly pleads that it is an august assembly of learned persons devoted to the performance of sacrifices and equal to Indra. They deserve to be respected and so she cannot stand before them in that sorry state. She begs Duhshasana not to drag and uncover her thus. She warns that her husbands, the Pandavas, will never forgive him in the future. Why she wonders, doesn't anyone, including the Kaurava elders, such as Bhishma, Vidura, and Drona stop Duhshasana? How can they remain silent spectators to this crime? Any other woman would have been distraught and hysterical at such a time but Draupadi, certainly agitated and anguished, remains in full control. She continues to ask her questions and taunt the moral sense of those present. She looks at the Pandavas who are inflamed with wrath at her plight but are forced to restrain themselves.

Karna, who is otherwise righteous, approves of Duhshasana's action. He is now avenging himself of Draupadi humiliating him at her *swayamvara* where she bluntly refused to accept him as her husband because of his low birth, even if he fulfilled the condition laid down by her father. Bhishma's moral bankruptcy and clinging on to the throne that he has presumably sacrificed becomes evident when, instead of stopping the abhorring molestation of a daughter-in-law in the open court by her brother-in-law, he merely murmurs that dharma is subtle and that is why he cannot answer the question Draupadi has raised. On the one hand, he says, a person who has no wealth cannot stake another's but, on the other hand, he concludes, wives are always under the orders and at the disposal of their husbands. Yudhishthira, he prevaricates, must have acted rightly as it was well known that he could abandon the whole world but never sacrifice morality. Knowing that he is unequal to Shakuni in dice he voluntarily played and staked Draupadi. Yudhishthira himself does to seem to think that Shakuni has played deceitfully as he has not protested even once. Therefore, says Bhishma, he is unable to decide upon the point raised by Draupadi.

Undaunted, Draupadi replies courageously that the King Yudhishthira has been summoned to the assembly although he has no skill in dice playing and has been made to play with wicked, deceitful, and desperate gamblers. How can he then be said to have staked anything voluntarily? She says that this wise assembly of the Kurus should reflect upon her words and duly decide the point she has placed before them.

Bhima, seeing Draupadi's plight, raves angrily against Yudhishthira, but he is restrained by his other brothers. After all, one of the aims of the Kauravas is also to create dissension among them and thus weaken their strength. Truth, however, has strange ways of manifesting itself. Where the wise patriarch Bhishma prevaricates and falters, Vikarna, Dhritarashtra's son, intervenes. He asks the assembled kings to answer the question raised by Yajnaseni (Draupadi), because if they do not, they will all be punished to rot in hell. Why is it that Bhishma and Dhritarashtra, the elders of the Kurus, and the ones with all the authority, and the great Vidura, do not say anything? The great acharyas, Drona and Kripa, are there too; why don't they answer according to their individual judgements, leaving aside all motives of profit and anger? Vikarna thus repeatedly appeals to those present in the assembly, but no one speaks. He then says that whether the others respond or not he will speak according to his judgement on what he thinks is just and proper. It has been said that hunting, drinking, gambling, and too much enjoyment of women, are the four vices of kings. Any man who is addicted to these is not considered virtuous and is not respected by his people. Yudhishthira too, has engaged in one of these vicious acts and urged by deceitful gamblers, staked the innocent Draupadi who is the common wife of all the Pandavas. Reflecting on all these circumstances, he says that he does not consider Draupadi to have been fairly won by the Kauravas.

Many in the assembly applaud Vikarna but Karna chastises him harshly. He pointedly refers to Draupadi as unchaste because she has several husbands. Hence, he says, it is all right to bring her to the assembly in one piece of cloth, and even to uncover her. The Pandavas themselves, together with Draupadi and all their wealth, have been 'won' by Duryodhana in the game of dice. Viciously, Karna orders Duhshasana to disrobe her and remove the garments of the Pandavas. Hearing this the Pandavas take off their upper garments and throwing them aside sit down in the assembly as slaves. Duhshasana then forcibly seizes Draupadi's attire, before the eyes of all, and begins to drag it off her person.

Having been so hopelessly let down by her husbands, and by the elders in the court, Draupadi thinks of her one true friend and saviour, Sri Krishna, and cries out to him, prays to him to save her from this humiliation. Although not present physically, Sri Krishna hears her prayers and covers her with an infinite spread of cloth. There is a story popularly attached to this episode. When Yudhishthira and the Pandavas performed the Rajasuya Yagna at Khandavaprastha, and as Sri Krishna threw his Sudarshana Chakra at Shishupala to behead him, his finger was injured, and it started bleeding. Seeing Sri Krishna's bleeding finger, Draupadi tore off a piece of cloth from her upper garment and bandaged it. Sri Krishna declared that he is ever indebted to her for this act of kindness and for each thread of the piece of garment used to bandage his finger. Thus, he repays the debt and bestows her the endless cloth covering to protect her modesty. The relationship between Sri Krishna and Draupadi is an indefinable one of a 'sakha'. He is her one true friend, her protector, an emotional anchor always, her "all in all". There is an underlying touch of romance, but it is really the highest kind of selfless trust and friendship that one can have in another being.

Quivering with anger at Draupadi's outrage, Bhima swears that he will take revenge for this humiliation by tearing open Duhshasana's breast in battle and drinking his blood. The kings present, beholding this extraordinary sight, applaud Draupadi's moral strength and censure Duhshasana for his shameless act. They also condemn Dhritarashtra for not answering the question raised by Draupadi. Vidura points out that Draupadi's outrage is a horrible violation of all norms of decency and morality. The law is unambiguously clear that when an aggrieved person like her approaches an assembly of good men and asks about her rights, those present are duty-bound to impartially answer her questions. Vikarna has given an answer according to his judgement, but others must respond as well, otherwise they are abetting injustice. Even then no one speaks. Karna orders Duhshasana to take Draupadi away.

Draupadi asks him to wait as she has something to do before she leaves the assembly. With superb irony she says that as she had been dragged there, she could not salute her seniors when she came in but that she will do so now that she is leaving, thus making them fully aware of the enormity of what they have done. She says that only once before, during her *swayamvara*, had she been seen by the assembled kings in the amphitheatre. But this time she has been dishonoured and humiliated. She reminds the elders that she is the daughter-in-law of the Kauravas and therefore, in effect they have lost their own prestige. She is also not merely the daughter-in-law of a king but is herself high born, being the daughter of a King. What can be more humiliating for her than to be so dragged to the public court? Where is the famed virtue of the Kuru Kings? Kings certainly do not allow their wives to be bandied about in a public court but that custom, she sarcastically remarks, seems to have disappeared from among the Kauravas. She is the wedded wife of King Yudhishthira, who hails from the same dynasty to which King Dhritarashtra and Duryodhana belong. She wants to know, whose serving woman is she supposed to be? She is determined to get an answer to her question on whether she is to be regarded as won or not, and will accept the verdict, whatever it might be, but someone there must give her an answer.

Bhishma once again falters and fumbles. The other kings present do not utter a word from fear of Duryodhana. On seeing this, Duryodhana takes Machiavellian delight at the situation, smiles, and to the discomfiture of the Pandavas, tells Draupadi that the question she has put depends on her husbands. Let the brothers declare that Yudhishthira is not their lord and prove him a liar. She will then be freed from slavery. Let Yudhishthira, who is the illustrious son of Dharma, himself declare whether he is her husband or not. Accordingly, he says, she should accept either the Pandavas or the Kauravas without delay. Some Kings applaud Duryodhana's stratagem, but others are distressed and look to Yudhishthira to bring the embarrassing situation to a satisfactory end. Bhima cannot restrain himself and bursts out saying that Yudhishthira is their lord is amply evident as otherwise there is no mortal creature on earth who could have escaped him after touching the hair of the princess of Panchala. He is bound by the ties of virtue and reverence due to their eldest brother and, repeatedly urged by Arjuna, he is not doing anything terrible, he warns. But if commanded by Yudhishthira even once, he will slay the sons of Dhritarashtra immediately.

Hearing Bhima, Duryodhana once again addresses Yudhishthira who sits in shocked silence and asks him to answer the question whether he regards Draupadi as won by the Kauravas or not. Insultingly, he uncovers his left thigh and commands Draupadi to sit on it. At this, Bhima vows to break Duryodhana's thigh in the battle, to avenge Draupadi. Vidura tries to make everybody realize the great danger and threat of devastation that is now rising from the wrath of Bhima and the Pandavas. He advises the Kauravas not to persist because an assembly devoid of virtue or ethics is polluted. If Yudhishthira had staked Draupadi before he himself was won, he would have certainly been her lord. Even Shakuni concedes that when a person stakes anything that he is himself incapable of holding, to win it is very like obtaining wealth in a dream. Listening to the words of the King of Gandhara, Vidura advises the

Kauravas to not overlook this unquestionable truth. Finally, just as the overwrought Draupadi threatens to curse the entire assembly with destruction, Gandhari rushes in, pleads and stops her.

The game of dice and the attempted disrobing of Draupadi are the turning points that make the war inevitable. These episodes persistently pose the question whether it is indeed a just war and whether the battlefield is finally the place where righteousness can be judged or decided. This is how Draupadi becomes central to the narrative. Otherwise, the *Mahabharata* would merely have been a battle of succession between two branches of a clan or family. Draupadi's question and the treatment meted out to her make her the pivot on which the wheels of war turn as urgent issues of righteousness and justice get involved and those are way beyond the mere settlement of dispute for the throne. Even if the accession issue had been settled with the endeavours of peace-making that were made before it, the war would still have been fought because of Draupadi's cry for justice. It is therefore not paradoxical that while Sri Krishna makes all efforts with talks of peace to avoid the war, he unfalteringly assures Draupadi later that she will be avenged, and the wives of the Kauravas would weep over the corpses of their husbands.

Ambiguities of dharma

Here we come to the ambiguities and paradoxes of dharma or righteousness and truth. Dharma works at different levels, is elusive and multifaceted. At the most technical level, the *Mahabharata* war is considered a *Dharmayudha* because it is being fought according to a code of conduct to which both sides have agreed. This is one, and in a sense, limited meaning of dharma. At the beginning of the battle, the rules of warfare are enumerated and accepted by both sides. These are universally accepted norms on humanitarian grounds and prevail in any civilized society. Among them are:

- Nobody will fight and kill someone who is running away from the battlefield
- Nobody must attack an unarmed and defenceless person.
- Fighting must be among equals.
- A charioteer can only fight a charioteer.
- A horseman confronts only another horseman.

However, these rules are blatantly violated by both sides at crucial moments during the war. On the Kaurava side, the single-handed defenceless Abhimanyu is brutally killed by seven warriors together, led by Dronacharya. Thereafter, Drona slays the fleeing Pandava soldiers indiscriminately, just before his death. Ashwatthama senselessly butchers the Pandava sons while they sleep, in the final brutality. On the Pandava side as well, dharma is violated several times – the slaying of Jayadratha, the felling of Bhishma with the help of Sikhandin, the killing of the defenceless Karna, the beheading of Drona by Dhrishtadyumna on Yudhishthira's uttering a lie that Ashwatthama is dead and Bhima defeating Duryodhana in the mace duel by breaking his thigh. Hence, the *Dharmayudha* degenerates into an *Adharmayudha* soon enough in the heat of the battle when victory at any cost is at stake.

It is Draupadi's humiliation that tilts the balance in favour of the Pandavas. As a war of succession both sides have ample justification to regard it as a just war. On the one hand, if Dhritarashtra was removed from the throne due to his blindness surely that could not extinguish the rights of the eldest son, Duryodhana? For Yudhishthira, since his father Pandu ascended the throne, the line of succession has to deviate from Dhritarashtra and pass on to Pandu's sons. This tenuous claim could be easily challenged. In any case, Pandu may have become the king, but his rule was short-lived, and it was Dhritarashtra who ruled over Hastinapura for the longest time, making his eldest son's claim even stronger. From his point of view, he had been magnanimous enough to accommodate Yudhishthira and his brothers at Khandavaprastha. Hence the claims of justice and righteousness are ambiguous on the side of the Pandavas as Duryodhana repeatedly asserts. The last and horrifying straw, therefore, is the unacceptable humiliation of Draupadi, the attempt to molest a sister-in-law by a brother-in-law, with the active connivance and encouragement of the father-in-law, in front the whole assembly. This utterly reprehensible act, the lowest point ethically that could be reached, must be avenged and on this count the war must be fought, and the Pandavas must win, as Sri Krishna repeatedly points out and finally ensures.

FEARFUL AMENDMENTS: After the violation of decency and decorum in the court of the Hastinapura, evil omens occur immediately and Dhritarashtra, suddenly fearing that his destruction is near at hand, and just as Draupadi is ready to curse the entire assemblage, he hastens to make amends, especially after Gandhari intervenes. He begins to console Draupadi by letting her ask for any boon that she may desire. Draupadi wishes for Yudhishthira to be freed from slavery as she does not want her son from him, Prativindhya, to be known as the son of a slave. Dhritarashtra readily accedes to this and allows her another boon. She wishes Bhima, Dhananjaya, and the twins to be freed together with their chariots and weapons. Granting this too, Dhritarashtra lets her ask for a third boon which she declines because she feels that freed from bondage, her husbands will achieve prosperity by their own courage and valour.

Despite his earlier venomous outbursts against her, Karna is filled with admiration for Draupadi. He has never seen a beautiful woman achieve so much and with such dignity. She single-handedly provides reprieve for her husbands in a situation that is so completely hostile and was loaded against her moments before. Bhima is enraged when he hears Karna say that they have been saved by their wife, but again, Arjuna calms him down. Bhima wants to slay all the foes assembled there but Yudhishthira pacifies him and turns to Dhritarashtra to ask him what is to be done next. Dhritarashtra returns their kingdom and all their wealth and tells them to go and rule peacefully. He begs them to forget the harsh words spoken to them, his own role in the entire episode of the game of dice, and the events that followed. He advises peace. Yudhishthira takes leave and sets out with his brothers and Draupadi to Khandavaprastha. But matters have obviously not been concluded on either side. Draupadi's insult cannot be ignored and Duryodhana is certainly not ready to reconcile to sharing the kingdom.

EXILED TO THE FOREST: On learning that Dhritarashtra has allowed the Pandavas to go back to their kingdom with Draupadi, Duhshasana immediately rushes to Duryodhana and despondently relates that all that they have won from the Pandavas has also been lost because of the folly of their father. At this, Duryodhana, Karna, and Shakuni hasten to see Dhritarashtra privately so that they can immediately counter this move before it is too late. They swarn him that by letting the Pandavas go, he has endangered all of them as they, the Pandavas, are sure to take revenge. They suggest that Dhritarashtra invites them to one more game of dice, and once and for all settle the issue of succession to the throne. Either the Kauravas or the Pandavas will win in the one crucial decisive game. The only wager in the game would be twelve years' exile into the forests with the thirteenth year of exile to be spent incognito in some other inhabited country. If the identity of the exiled party is discovered in the final year, the whole cycle of exile will be repeated. Dhritarashtra orders that the Pandavas be brought back and once again be asked to cast dice. When this 'invitation' or 'command' to play comes, the one thing that Draupadi asks of Yudhishthira, "Please do not wager your brothers or me." When the Pandavas return to play again the one-point wager is explained. As is to be expected, the Pandavas lose. Hence, they prepare for exile, accompanied by Draupadi while Kunti stays back; significantly, not at the Hastinapura palace but in the kingdom, with Vidura. No other wives of the Pandavas accompany them.

Draupadi now takes on the role that Kunti has performed all her life. Like her mother-in-law, she is always the queen whether in the palace or in the forest and performs her duties accordingly. She holds the Pandavas together as Kunti has done earlier and keeps their sights focused on the throne. She vows not to bind her tresses till she has washed them with Duhshasana's blood, thus keeping the memory of her humiliation alive and forestalling any thought that they might ever have of rapprochement and reconciliation.

On hearing that the Pandavas have been banished, the Bhojas, Vrishnis, Andhakas, the king of Chedis, and the celebrated and the powerful brothers, the Kaikeyes, head out to meet them in the forest. Draupadi takes every opportunity to draw attention to what has happened with her and pleads for war. She complains to Sri Krishna, tracing the history of Duryodhana's animosity towards the Pandavas. While they were children, Duryodhana mixed poison in Bhima's food who managed to digest it. He bound the unsuspecting and sleeping Bhima and threw him into the River Ganga, but waking up from sleep, Bhima had torn his bonds and risen from the water.

It was Duryodhana who had caused a black cobra to bite Bhima, but again he survived. It was Duryodhana who had planned to burn down the Pandavas together with Kunti, their mother, in the house of lac in Varnavata, forcing them to escape and live in the forest for years, in hiding. But for Bhima who had carried his brothers and mother in his arms and on his back and had leaped out of the burning house they would not be alive.

They had had to face untold hardships and dangers then, as they moved from place to place concealing their identity. She wants Sri Krishna's protection as her friend. Yet again, she gets the desired response and the promise from him that the Kauravas will be destroyed. Vasudeva comforts the grieving Draupadi and assures her that the wives of those who insulted her in the assembly of heroic warriors would weep seeing their husbands lying dead on the ground, their bodies covered with Arjuna's arrows. He commits his support to the Pandavas and says that Draupadi would certainly be their queen. Hearing this, Draupadi looks obliquely at Arjuna for confirmation, and he too promises that it would be as Sri Krishna has said. Dhrishtadyumna vows to slay Drona and Sikhandin is destined to cause Bhishma's death. Bhima's targets are Duryodhana and Duhshana, Arjuna's is Karna. Nakul and Sahadeva are not going to spare Shakuni and his progeny.

DRAUPADI AND YUDHISHTHIRA'S REFLECTIONS: Exiled to the woods, Yudhishthira and Draupadi often talk about what has befallen them, why it has happened, how to cope with it, and what should be the future course of action. Draupadi continuously keeps the spirits of the Pandavas up and will not let them, particularly Yudhishthira, sink into a fatalistic acceptance of their situation. Draupadi reminds Yudhishthira that Duryodhana has felt no sorrow in depriving them of their right and consigning them to the hardships of the forests. Duryodhana, Karna, Shakuni, and Duhshasana are the only people who do not mourn their departure. All the other Kurus and the people of the kingdom are filled with sorrow. Draupadi goads Yudhishthira on by saying that she feels sorry for him and regrets the state to which he has fallen. She appeals to his love for his brothers by pointing out that her heart knows no peace seeing Bhimasena and the others living in the woods. A Kshatriya, she reminds him, who does not find his courage when the opportunity rises, is disregarded by all. Therefore, forgiveness is unbecoming of Yudhishthira. He should realize that there is a time to forgive and a time to fight and act.

Draupadi then proceeds to inspire Yudhishthira by narrating to him the story of Prahlada and Vali, the son of Virochana. One day, Vali asks his wise grandfather, Prahlada, whether forgiveness is meritorious or might and courage are. Prahlada replies that taken exclusively, neither might nor forgiveness, is meritorious. He who always forgives suffers many wrongs as no one ever respects him. Unscrupulous people try to exploit him and deprive him of his wealth. They try to rob him of his vehicles, clothes, ornaments, and other belongings. They even desire his wife and the wife, too, tends to go astray. But those who never forgive also suffer. They get separated from their friends and are hated both by relatives and strangers. A man who insults others loses his wealth, is discarded and hated, suffers grief, and makes many enemies. He is in danger of losing his property and even his life. He who equally threatens both his friends and enemies is an object of alarm in the world and can, therefore, never achieve prosperity. Therefore, men must use their discretion and be neither excessively aggressive nor ever-forgiving.

Draupadi then goes on to enunciate some rules:

- One who has served should be forgiven even if on some occasion he has done a wrong.
- Those who act in ignorance should also be forgiven as all men do not have learning or wisdom.
- Those who offend knowingly must be punished even if their offence be trivial.
- A first offence should be forgiven.
- The second time around punishment is essential even if the offence be trivial.
- If, however, a person has unwillingly offended, he should be pardoned after a judicious enquiry.
- Humility vanquishes both might and weakness.
- Sometimes offenders need to be forgiven for fear of repercussions.
- At other times they must not be spared.

Therefore, there is no absolute rule to follow. All acts must be judged with reference to time and place, taking into consideration strengths and weaknesses of the one performing the act. With this lesson, it is evident that Draupadi is a master of statecraft.

KARMA AND DHARMA: Draupadi urges Yudhishthira to demonstrate his strength as the time has come for it. Yudhishthira, however, is not convinced and counsels patience as no action should be taken in anger, he opines. Yudhishthira explains to Draupadi, that without forgiveness there can be no peace on earth. If all those who are injured take revenge, existence itself will be in jeopardy. If kings give way to wrath, their subjects will be destroyed. Forgiveness and gentleness are the qualities of a self-possessed person, says Yudhishthira. Hence, Yudhishthira talks of peace and forgiveness while Draupadi advocates war. Citing Kashyapa, Yudhishthira says, forgiveness means sacrifice and peace is divine. He is aware and realizes nonetheless that a crisis has enveloped the history of the Bharatas, and they stand on the brink of calamity.

Draupadi finds Yudhishthira's arguments delusory, as she says that men find themselves in different situation because of their actions because actions inevitably lead to consequences. Men are unable to attain prosperity by virtue, gentleness, forgiveness, straightforwardness, and fear of censure. Yudhishthira's own sufferings prove this because he does not really deserve them. Nothing is dearer to him than dharma and he can abandon everything and everyone, including his brothers and herself for it, but he has been cheated and deceived by his Kaurava brothers. She has heard that a king protects virtue and is protected by it, but this does not seem to have been the case with Yudhishthira. Irritated by his continuous harping on virtue and peace, she lashes out and asks what perversity attracted him towards gambling. Perhaps he can blame everything on destiny because then it can be said that men do not act according to their own volition. They are fated to do so according to the will of God and remain puppets in His hand. Hence their well-being or otherwise depends only on God and they are not responsible. But in that case, God Himself seems to be arbitrary, creating and destroying creatures at will, sometimes behaving like a kind parent and at other times like a vicious and wrathful person. Many honest people are persecuted while the sinful are happy.

Yudhishthira reproves Yajnaseni for propagating atheism. He says that he has never cared for the fruits of his actions for himself. He gives away what he can because it is his duty to do so as a person leading a domestic life. He only acts to do his duty and to follow the conduct of the good and wise. His heart, he says, is naturally attracted towards virtue and he regards the person who acts for reward as a mere trader in virtue. A doubting person also does not gain from his actions because of his scepticism. He who doubts the relevance of religion is miserable and is filled with anxieties. Even in the hereafter, such a person does not acquire regions of bliss as religion and dharma are the only support for going to heaven. Actions however, set into motion their own chain of effects or consequences. If the actions of the virtuous, emphasizes Yudhishthira, did not bear fruit, the universe would be enveloped in darkness. No one would then pursue salvation, seek to acquire knowledge or even wealth; and men would live like beasts. If asceticism, austerities of celibate life, sacrifice, charity, honesty are all meaningless, then human beings would not have practiced virtue generation after generation. If all virtuous acts were fruitless, there would be dire confusion. Therefore, even if fruits of virtue are not evident, religion or the gods must not be doubted. One should willingly perform sacrifices and practice charity with humility. He thus tries to refute what Draupadi is advocating and inspire her to faith.

Draupadi protests that she is not trying to disregard God or dharma but is only trying to make Yudhishthira act. Every conscious creature in this world, she asserts, must act as he or she is an animate being. Only those without consciousness, and are inanimate, do not act. Lives of all living beings are determined by their actions in former lives, but only human beings can influence the future course of their life with their actions. Without action, life is impossible. Therefore, Draupadi urges Yudhishthira that he must act irrespective of the outcome. Those who believe solely in destiny or chance, she asserts, are the worst, the weakest or most helpless among men and will be eventually destroyed. If a person gets wealth by chance, it is regarded as merely providential, and no credit is given to him. Only a person who acquires it through his own actions is respected as an able being. Every act or *karma* has consequences for the future lives, just as many things in this life are the consequences of actions in former lives. God, the Ordainer, distributes among men their portions according to what they have done in their past lives. The body is only God's instrument for doing action. Man has to first settle some purpose in his mind and then accomplish it by working with the aid of his intelligence. Thus, she argues, it could be said that man himself is the cause of what he does. Otherwise, he can neither be censured nor praised.

Draupadi encourages and boosts up Yudhishthira by saying that although misery has overtaken them at that time, they can overcome it but only if he will act. No one can foretell the consequences of his actions. Those can only be known or seen after the action has been performed. If, despite action, a person fails he cannot be blamed and therefore has no reason to reproach himself. She urges Yudhishthira not to despair if he fails despite acting, because God and chance governed by former lives also play their part. Since success depends on the coming together of many circumstances, it may or may not be commensurate to the action. But if there is no action, there can be no success in any case.

DRAUPADI'S PRIDE: While the Pandavas are in the forests, Sri Krishna and Satyabhama visit them. Draupadi and Satyabhama meet after a long time and immediately sit down to talk. Satyabhama is most impressed by the way the Pandavas look up to Draupadi and so asks her how she manages to rule over the sons of Pandu who have so much strength and beauty. How are they so obedient to her and never angry? Draupadi replies that she is the pivot of the existence of the Pandava brothers by her own severe endeavours and lack of jealousy. She never speaks a false or harsh word, nor does she ever give the brothers any cause for envy. She is the first to get up and the last to sleep. Ever attentive to her husbands, she keeps the household clean without ever showing any fatigue or irritation.

She worships the household gods and is always busy in work. She earlier served Kunti as selflessly and fulfilled the responsibilities given to her with respect to relatives and performance of charity. Also, she has always done everything expected of her as the wife of King Yudhishthira. She advises Satyabhama to do the same.

In an amusing variation from eighteenth-century Bengal, a story has been accrued to the *Mahabharata* in which Draupadi's pride at her being an ideal wife, entirely dedicated to her five Pandava husbands, is crushed. It is a very humane story, the fundamentals of which might echo in many a heart. As the thirteenth year of their exile in the forest is approaching, when the Pandavas and Draupadi would have to live incognito, Yudhishthira tells Draupadi that they ought to leave Kamyaka forest where they had been living so far, and go elsewhere, otherwise Duryodhana will keep pursuing them, making it impossible for them to conceal their identities. So, they leave and on the second day they reach the Kamya Lake where they rest. Yajnaseni thinks that in all the three worlds there is no one like her in being so entirely devoted to her husbands, accompanying them in the forests and being with them in all their dangers, sorrows, and grief. In a self-congratulatory mode, she thinks of her fame and how widely she is acclaimed. Sri Krishna understands her thoughts and decides to crush her pride.

The Pandavas come upon a lovely ashrama full of fruit trees when Draupadi sees there a mango growing out of season. She asks Arjuna to get it for her, which he promptly does by shooting an arrow to bring it down. Just then Sri Krishna appears and says that surely destiny has led to them to their destruction through this mango. This ashrama belongs to Rishi Sandipan and both the gods and the demons tremble at his name. He goes away every morning to perform his austerities; but when he returns in the evening, he eats this one mango, which he grows daily for his evening meal. Not finding the mango, he will be so angry that he will reduce everybody to ashes.

Yudhishthira fold his hands and pleads with Sri Krishna to save them. The latter says that the fruit can be re-joined to the branch if each of them speaks the truth and tells him what always crosses their minds. All agree to do so. Yudhishthira speaks first. He says that he constantly thinks that if he regains his property, he will perform Yajna day and night. Bhima says that he constantly thinks of the day when he will rip open Duhshasana's breast with his nails and drink his blood, and when he will break Duryodhana's thigh. Arjuna wants to acquire innumerable weapons for the war and slay Karna with his arrows. Nakula wants Yudhishthira to be installed on the throne of Hastinapura while he himself will be the crown prince and report to him the good and ill happening in the kingdom. Sahdeva similarly desires to serve Yudhishthira when he becomes king and serve Kunti while looking after the citizens.

As each of the brothers speaks truthfully from the heart, the fruit rises higher and higher and almost reaches the tip of the branch from where it has been severed. Then Draupadi says that day and night she dreams that all the Kauravas will be slain by Bhima and their women will weep in sorrow. She herself will perform a great Yajna as before and look after all friends and relatives. As soon as Draupadi says this, the fruit plummets to the ground indicating that she has not spoken the truth. They all plead with her to say what is actually on her mind so that they will not be destroyed by the wrath of the rishi. But she remains silent. On Yudhishthira's pleading, Draupadi reveals that when she saw Karna, she thought that if only he had been the son of Kunti she would have had six husbands and that thought had come to her mind when she was asking for the fruit. As soon as Draupadi speaks out, the fruit shoots up and gets fixed on to the branch. Yudhishthira becomes silent and Bhima berates her, declaring her untrustworthy in all aspects. Sri Krishna, however, calms him down and tells him to stop slandering Draupadi. He reminds the brothers that there is no one like Draupadi and he knows why she is attracted to Karna, but he will not tell them till Yudhishthira regains the throne. The reason, of course, is what gets revealed later, that Karna is actually Kunti's son and the elder brother of the Pandavas. Perhaps Draupadi was instinctively attracted because he was one of the sons of Kunti and hence the brother of the Pandavas. If this had been known earlier, he would have also been her husband. However, Draupadi's satisfied smugness is decisively shattered.

CHALLENGES: Draupadi is always the queen and has to act as such. Sometimes this leads to difficult situations, especially when an attempt is made to harm the Pandavas. Duryodhana sends Durvasa Rishi, known for his quick temper, together with his ten thousand disciples to where the Pandavas are living in the woods. He is aware that by then Draupadi will have finished her meal and cleaned the copper utensil, the *Akshaya patra*, given to them by Surya, which is blessed to always contain food till she eats her meal, after feeding the others. This being the case Draupadi will be unable to provide food to Durvasa and his entourage. If she fails in the duty of feeding the visitors, the sage will undoubtedly curse them. Draupadi prays to Sri Krishna and asks for his protection just as he saved her earlier from Duhshasana. Hearing her prayers, Sri Krishna immediately arrives and demands food from her saying that he is very hungry. At this Draupadi gets very confused and irritated given that there is no more food in the vessel, and she is facing a crisis. Madhava tells her to bring the vessel to him. He looks in and finds a grain of rice and vegetable sticking at its rim. He puts that in his mouth and says, in a very satisfied tone, that he is satiated. He then asks Bhima to invite the Rishis to dinner. But thanks to Sri Krishna's divine intervention, Rishi Durvasa and the other rishis having finished their baths, also feel equally satiated and hastily leave. Yudhishthira and Draupadi are saved from the embarrassing situation.

DRAUPADI'S VULNERABILITY: Draupadi's beauty and wit make her very vulnerable. After the horror in the Hastinapura court, there are two instances of her being sexually assaulted — once when Jayadratha tries to abduct her and then when Kichaka tries to overpower and seduce her. They parallel the assault post the game of dice. Yudhishthira constantly fails her, but the other brothers circumvent his orders and avenge her in their own way. In the Jayadratha episode, they do not kill him because Yudhishthira forbids them, but they certainly humiliate him. In the case of Kichaka, Bhima does not consult Yudhishthira and slaughters him. This also foreshadows Kunti's advice to her sons to go to war after the period of exile has ended and negotiations have failed. While she concentrates mainly on motivating Yudhishthira, she also openly suggests that if he does not agree, they should follow Draupadi's advice and not his.

While the Pandavas live in the great forest of Kamyaka, Jayadratha, the King of Sindhu, is passing by on his way to the kingdom of Salva, dressed in his best royal apparel and accompanied by numerous princes, with a view to matrimony. He halts in the woods of Kamyaka and in that secluded place he sees Draupadi standing alone on the threshold of the hermitage as the Pandavas have gone hunting. Her beauty makes every other woman pale in comparison. Jayadratha is struck with amazement at the sight of her and inflamed with desire, is now determined to marry her. Draupadi tells him who she is and chides him, saying that it is not proper for him to speak thus to her. Despite her protests, Jayadratha forcibly abducts her. Sage Dhaumya tries to intervene, but to no avail.

Meanwhile, the Pandavas gather at one place after hunting in different directions. Yudhishthira realizes that something is terribly wrong as the birds and wild beasts are flying towards the sunset uttering dissonant cries and displaying intense excitement, indicating that the forest has been invaded by hostile intruders. He himself is uneasy and feels that they should return hastily to their hermitage. When they reach there, they find Draupadi's maid Dhatreyika, sobbing and weeping. They anxiously inquire after Draupadi, determined to rescue her from whatever harm that may have befallen her. Dhatreyika informs them that Jayadratha has forcibly carried her away and urges them to go quickly and rescue her. They immediately depart and find Dhaumya who is also trying to follow Jayadratha. They catch up with Jayadratha, defeat him and bring him to Yudhishthira who himself has not given the chase but has instructed his brothers to do so. He has warned them that Jayadratha should only be captured and not killed as he is Dushala's husband, who was the Kaurava's sister hence like their sister. Once again Draupadi's abuse takes a backseat over other considerations. However, Bhima is overwhelmed with wrath at what Jayadratha has done to Draupadi. Unable to go against Yudhishthira's command of not killing him, he humiliates Jayadratha by shaving off his head leaving only five tufts of hair, a clear indication to any perceiver that the tonsure is a punishment meted out to him. Bhima also tells him that if he wishes to stay alive then he must proclaim in public assemblies and open courts that he is the slave of Pandavas. That is the customary rule of conquest on the battlefield. Jayadratha has no choice but to agree. Arjuna and Bhima bind him and present him in this condition to Yudhishthira and Draupadi. Yudhishthira tells his brothers to set Jayadratha free. Draupadi naturally feels immensely incensed but reading her husband's mind, concurs, as she has no choice but to agree. While Yudhishthira has not avenged her, Bhima and Arjuna have at least partially done so, by humiliating him. Warning Jayadratha, Yudhishthira lets him go.

In the thirteenth year of their exile, the Pandavas go to the kingdom of Virata and take up employment in the court, under disguise. Yudhishthira claims to be a Brahmin called Kanka, who has been a great friend of Yudhishthira and now offers to be Virata's companion. Bhima becomes Vallabha the cook and takes charge of the kitchen. Arjuna puts on female garb and declares himself to be the neuter Brihannala. He lives in the female apartments teaching Virata's daughter and her companions, music and dance. This is also the working out of the curse that the apsara Urvashi has put on him. When he was at Indra's court in the quest of celestial weapons, Urvashi, the beautiful celestial dancer, propositioned him. He turned her down saying that she had relations with his father Indra. Incensed, Urvashi cursed him that he would be a neuter for the rest of his life. When Indra heard about this, he chided Urvashi for her hasty and unthinking action, and modified the curse. It could not be totally annulled but he reduced it to a period of one year, knowing also that Arjuna would be able to put it to very valuable use. Hence, Arjuna as Brihannala, lives in Virata's harem for a year. Nakula, as Granthika, becomes the keeper of Virata's horses and Sahdeva, as Tantripala, becomes the keeper of the cattle. Draupadi presents herself to be a Sairindhri, skilled in dressing hair, and offers to serve the queen Sudeshna. She claims to have waited on Queen Draupadi. Yudhishthira warns her to be on guard against the lecherous eyes of men while she works in that position. He is aware that Draupadi's unparalleled beauty, even when modestly dressed as Sairindhri, cannot be veiled. Queen Sudeshna herself worries that if the females of her household and her maids find her so attractive, then the king himself might be smitten by her. Which male could resist her attraction? King Virata, she fears, might forsake her on seeing Draupadi. Of course, Draupadi reassures her saying that neither Virata nor any other person can influence her as she has five youthful Gandharvas as husbands; sons of an exceedingly powerful Gandharva king, and they will always protect her. No one can do her any harm. She then proceeds to lay down conditions of her employment, saying that her husbands wish her to serve only such persons who will not make her eat food already partaken by another or expect her to wash their feet. She warns that anyone who attempts to lay even a finger on her will be killed by them that very night as the Gandharvas always protect her secretly. Sudeshna is delighted to hear this and agrees to her conditions. Thus, Draupadi begins to live in the court of Virata.

Under their respective disguises, the Pandavas spend all the time of the year of living incognito in Virata's city, quietly, although impatiently. Draupadi, too, passes her days in misery at Sudeshna's beck and call. Just as the year is about to end, Kichaka, the commander of Virata's forces, happens to enter his sister, Queen Sudeshna's chambers, and sets eyes on Draupadi. He is at once mad with desire and wants to possess her at any cost. He propositions her and even offers to make her his queen. When she refuses, Kichaka's anger knows no bounds. He threatens her with dire consequences boasting that he is the real lord of the kingdom and not Virata. Draupadi warns him not to act in haste and thereby jeopardize his life. She has the protection of her five Gandharva husbands therefore, what he is asking for is impossible. Her Gandharva husbands certainly will kill him, she warns.

Blinded and maddened by lust, the rejected Kichaka tells his sister Sudeshna to find a way so that he can enjoy Sairindhari. Moved by her brother's pleas, Sudeshna tells him to find an occasion to procure food and wine so that she will send

Sairindhari to him on the pretext of fetching it for her. And, when Sairindhari comes to him in solitude, he can do what he likes with her. Sudeshna then asks Sairindhri to go to Kichaka's palace, as planned. Draupadi refuses saying that she fears Kichaka's intentions. She is sure that Kichaka will insult her and hence she does not want to go. She reminds the queen of her the terms of service. But the queen persuades her saying that he will not misbehave with her once he knows that she has been sent by his sister. Saying this, she hands over a covered golden vessel to her. Filled with apprehension, Draupadi sets out for Kichaka's place. On the way, she worships Surya for a moment and Surya, seeing her situation, commands a *rakshasa* to invisibly protect her.

Kichaka is overjoyed to see Draupadi. He once again tells her to accept his demand and in return she will have all the jewellery and gems in the world. He will make her his queen and all his other wives will be her slaves. Draupadi reproves him and threatens that her husbands will leave him powerless on the ground. Kichaka seizes her by her garments and tries to force himself upon her. Unable to tolerate it anymore, trembling with wrath, she dashes him to the ground.

As Kichaka tumbles, she runs to Yudhishthira for protection. Kichaka pursues her, seizes her by the hair, brings her down on the ground, and kicks her in the very presence of both Yudhishthira and the king. Thereupon the *rakshasa* appointed by Surya to protect Draupadi, hurls Kichaka away with the force of a mighty wind. Both Yudhishthira and Bhima are present and see what has happened. Bhima is about to get up speedily when Yudhishthira restrains him fearing discovery of their identity. He tells Bhima to return to the kitchen and asks Draupadi to return to her quarters without making a fuss.

Draupadi sees that her husbands, compelled to keep their disguise, are helpless. She now proceeds to garner support for herself from others to help herself and to create disapproval and dissatisfaction for Virata among his own people. Boldly addressing Virata, the king of Matsyas, she says that Kichaka had dared to kick the wife of those whose foes could never sleep in peace even if four kingdoms intervened between. Her husbands, she said, were bound by ties of duty; otherwise, they could destroy the entire world.

Her anger spills over. She taunts Virata and wonders what she, a weak woman, can do, when the king himself allows an innocent person to be so wronged in front of his very eyes. She condemns him saying that he is behaving more like a robber than a king. She asks the courtiers to mark the violence that she has been subjected to because of a king, ignorant of duty and morality, and asserts that the courtiers who wait upon such a king share in the blame. Draupadi tries to get the courtiers on her side, to arouse them against Virata and she succeeds. When the courtiers learn of what has happened, they applaud Draupadi and praise her courage. Yudhishthira's brow is covered with sweat because of anger. Fearful that they will be discovered before time and then the 12-year exile would begin all over again, Yudhishthira has no option but to tell her to stop. He cannot protect her at this juncture, only give her advice. The wives of heroes, he hints obliquely, bear affliction for the sake of their husbands. But Draupadi replies sarcastically that they to whom she is married are all extremely kind but as the eldest of them is addicted to dice, they have no choice but to suffer oppression from all. Having said this, she runs towards Sudeshna's apartments. When Sudeshna comes to know what has happened, she is petrified and fears for her brother.

Wishing for Kichaka's destruction, Draupadi returns to her quarters and ponders on how he can be punished. She realizes that only Bhima can avenge her under the circumstances. She goes quickly to Bhima's quarter where he is asleep and coils herself around him. Aroused, Bhima wonders what could have happened. He is, of course, ready to do whatever she asks of him. Draupadi wonders how he can sleep after what has been perpetrated on her that day. As she embraces him, Bhima promises that he will avenge her. Finding out all the details he then persuades her to return speedily to her own apartments before others awake.

While giving Bhima the details, Draupadi buttresses her cause with emotional appeals. She says that she is not lamenting for herself alone. She cannot bear to see him as a cook, calling himself Vallabha, sunk in the servitude of Virata, who made him fight with elephants for his pleasure. She faints from anxiety for him on such occasions and is heart-broken to be taunted by the princesses who keep saying that Sairindhri is in love with Vallabha. Not only Bhima, but she also despairs to see the mighty Arjuna with his hair in braids living the life of a neuter amid women. Similarly, she hates the sight of Sahadeva tending Virata's cattle as a cowherd and Nakula training the horses. Living as a maid under Sudeshna's command in the guise of Sairindhri, she can only carry on in the hope that the period of their exile will soon come to an end. Success, victory, defeat, she philosophizes, are all transitory and prosperity she hopes will return to her husbands just as they have suffered adversity. Prosperity and misfortune are all experienced alternately as the wheel of time revolves and no one is immune to the ups and downs of life. No one also knows what causes grief or happiness. That which brings victory can also lead to defeat. Nothing is difficult for Destiny, and none can override it. Hence, she is waiting for the return of favourable fortune. Draupadi thus laments before Bhima laying everything at the door of Destiny if no one else will help her.

Bhima retorts that he would have killed Kichaka in the court and slaughtered the Matsyas there and then, but Yudhishthira forbade him with a glance. Understanding his intentions, he had kept quiet. The thought that they have been deprived of their kingdom and that he has not yet slain the

Kurus nor taken the head of Shakuni, is burning up every limb of his body. However, he advises her not to sacrifice virtue and to subdue her wrath. If King Yudhishthira hears such rebukes from her, he will end his life in remorse. If even Arjuna and the twins hear her speak thus, they will die. In the past, virtuous women like Indrasena, Sukanya, Sita, Lopamudra and others have followed their husbands patiently in adversity. Only half a month is left for their exile to be over and Draupadi cannot afford to lose her patience.

Hearing Bhima's words, Draupadi controls herself and admits that she has lamented only because she is unable to bear her grief. She does not intend to be harsh about Yudhishthira and in any case, there is no use of dwelling on the past. She says that queen Sudeshna, jealous of her beauty, has ill-treated her to prevent the king from taking a fancy to her. Kichaka constantly solicits her, knowing that his sister will be on his side and will be happy to see her suffer. That is why, despite knowing of Kichaka's intentions, Sudeshna sent her for wine to his place. She narrates all that has happened and says that the king has neither prevented Kichaka from trying to outrage her nor has he punished him. Kichaka, although adulterous and lecherous, is a favourite of both the king and the queen as they depend on him for the safety of their kingdom. If Kichaka sees her again he will certainly ravish her, and she will then be left with no choice but to renounce her life and die by taking poison. This clinches the argument for Bhima and he becomes determined to slay Kichaka. Bhima is now ready to take revenge no matter what Yudhishthira feels and whatever be the consequences.

Together Bhima and Draupadi draw up a plan. He tells Draupadi to lure Kichaka to the empty dancing hall alone at night and he will slay him there. Both wait impatiently for the proper moment. The following morning Kichaka accosts Draupadi and taunts her saying that since her husbands had not protected her when he had kicked her in the court, she should now accept him. Draupadi replies that she is ready to yield to him, and it has only been fear of her husbands that has prevented her. Kichaka is delighted and invites her to his home, but Draupadi convinces him to meet her in the dancing hall that night as the Gandharva do not know of that place, she explains.

Draupadi waits impatiently for nightfall and Kichaka spends the day preparing for the night. She informs Bhima that their plan is on course. Bhima is delighted and says he will get as much joy from it as he got earlier in killing Hidimba. After he has slain Kichaka he will later slay Duryodhana, and his revenge will then be complete. But Draupadi cautions him that Kichaka must be slain in secret.

When Kichaka comes to meet Draupadi at night, Bhima is waiting for him and slays him. He promises Draupadi that henceforth anyone who insults her will meet the same fate. He then returns to his quarters while Draupadi returns to hers, saying to the keepers of the dancing hall that Kichaka, who tried to violate her, has been slain by her Gandharva husbands.

All Kichaka's relatives come and grieve over him. Trouble brews as Yudhishthira anticipated and feared but, in this case, he has been kept in the dark. When Kichaka's clan sees his badly mangled body, they demand Draupadi's death as she is the cause of Kichaka's death. In their fury, they decide to forcibly cremate her with him as his last wish had been union with her. They appeal to Virata, who knowing the strength and power of Kichaka's clan, meekly gives his assent. So, they seize Draupadi and bind her by the waist to his bier and set out with determination to the cemetery while she cries out for help.

Bhima hears Draupadi's wails and without a moment's reflection starts up from his bed, and rushes to rescue her. Carefully, he changes his clothes and goes out of the palace from a different gate to proceed towards the funeral ground. He then fights and kills a hundred and six *sutas*, together with Virata's General. Seeing that astounding feat, men and women are filled with astonishment. They report to the king and tell him of what has happened, also saying that the Gandharvas have slain all the *sutas*. They proclaim that Sairindhri is the source of all the troubles as she is so extraordinarily beautiful and sensuous that no man can remain immune to her. The Gandharvas are exceedingly powerful and because of Sairindhri, Virata's kingdom is in danger. Hence, they appeal to the king to not only make proper funeral arrangements for the *sutas* but also to devise ways to protect the kingdom from the fury of the Gandharvas.

On hearing this, Virata tells his wife Sudeshna to get rid of Sairindhri and ask her to go away wherever she likes. Accordingly, the queen tells Draupadi or Sairindhri that the King is afraid after what has happened and so wants her to leave his kingdom immediately. Draupadi requests for thirteen days' time and says that the Gandharvas will also be highly obliged for this. This is, of course, a veiled threat and she knows that Virata has no choice but to accept this condition in his self-interest seeing the destruction that has already been caused.

On the thirteenth day, as the thirteenth year of exile incognito ends, the true identities of the Pandavas and Draupadi are revealed to an aghast and overwhelmed Virata. He readily and joyfully accepts the proposal of the marriage of his daughter Uttara with Abhimanyu, Arjuna's son by Subhadra.

*EXILE ENDS **and efforts to regain the kingdom begin***: Among others, Sri Krishna arrives in King Virata's palace. There is a conclave about the steps that need to be taken to enable the Pandavas to regain their kingdom and return to Hastinapura. As they ponder over the last peace proposal to be sent to Dhritarashtra and Duryodhana, Draupadi gets very disturbed. She is the only one who has accompanied the Pandavas in their misfortune. After all that she has suffered, the ultimate public humiliation, first in the Kuru court and twice later, she has been able to endure everything with only one burning desire in her heart, that one day her husbands will avenge her humiliation.

Hearing Yudhishthira's resolve to offer peace, Draupadi once again takes matters in her own hands and intervenes. Greatly aggrieved she once more appeals to Sri Krishna, saying that he knows how deceitfully Duryodhana and his advisors have robbed the Pandavas of their happiness. There is nothing left to negotiate as the Kauravas have never been amenable to reconciliation. The Pandavas together with their allies, the Srinjayas, will be able to withstand Dhritarashtra's army. Hence, Sri Krishna should inflict heavy punishment on the Kauravas to redeem the entire Kshatriya race. The covetous ought to be slain and there is no sin in destroying those who deserve it, declares Draupadi.

She further questions Sri Krishna, since she trusts him completely, and wants to know if there is any woman on the earth like her who would still be alive after enduring so much, in spite being born in a high family and being married into an even more famous one. She has five sons by these five heroes, all great warriors to whom Sri Krishna is morally bound, as he is to Abhimanyu. Yet, she was seized by the hair, dragged into the assembly and treated as a slave. When the Pandavas saw it and sat silently without giving way to their wrath, she had called upon Sri Krishna to save her, as he was her only friend.

Instead of getting protection from her husbands she got them their freedom. On her asking, Dhritarashtra restored their freedom, kingdom, wealth and weapons. But they were freed only to be exiled again to the woods because of another game of dice. Sri Krishna knows all her sorrow and hence she appeals to him to rescue her together with her husbands, kinsmen, and relatives and protect them from further grief. Morally, she is the daughter-in-law of both Bhishma and Dhritarashtra and yet she was forcibly made a slave to their sons. What is the use of Arjuna's marksmanship and Bhima's might if Duryodhana has lived even for a moment after her humiliation? If she deserves any justice, she insists that Sri Krishna's wrath must be directed towards the sons of Dhritarashtra.

Her eyes brimming with tears and emotionally charged, she takes her tresses in her left hand and walks towards Krishna saying that he, who is so anxious for peace with the enemy should, in all his acts, remember that her hair has been seized by Duhshasana's cruel hands and she will only bind it after she has washed it with his blood. Contemptuous of all peace proposals, she finally says that if Bhima and Arjuna have also become cowards so low as to yearn for peace, then her aged father and her brothers will avenge her in battle. Her courageous five sons, together with Abhimanyu, will fight with the Kauravas. What peace can her heart know unless she sees Duhshasana's arm crushed? Draupadi's voice chokes with tears and her body shakes with convulsive sobs.

Sri Krishna comforts her saying as he did earlier, that she would indeed see the Kaurava ladies weeping as she is now. They will surely lament the death of their relatives and friends because they, in fact, have "already been slain by him". Only the physical act waits to be accomplished by Bhima, Arjuna and the twins, at the command of Yudhishthira. If the sons of Dhritarashtra do not heed his words, they will surely die, and nothing can undo what he says. However, he counsels, she should not be impatient. Her enemies will certainly be destroyed, but the due process of peace-making must be followed. Draupadi gets Krishna's commitment to destroy their enemies. Comforting and assuring Draupadi of his support, Sri Krishna departs for Hastinapura for the last round of negotiations, which he knows are doomed to fail.

In the Hastinapura court, while Sri Krishna tries his utmost to make Dhritarashtra see the folly of their ways, and while berating Duryodhana, Sri Krishna says that apart from everything else, Duryodhana needs to be most severely punished for insulting his brother's wife, dragging her into the assembly, and addressing her in the worst kind of lowly language.

THE WAR AND ITS AFTERMATH: The war is finally fought, and it brings its own deep sorrows in its wake. At its end, it is again Draupadi who suffers the most on the side of the Pandavas as her sons are brutally slain by Ashwatthama, Kripa, and Kritavarman while they sleep peacefully in their camp, believing the war has been won. Satyaki escapes with great difficulty and brings the news to Yudhishthira. Yudhishthira's grief knows no bounds. He does not know how to tell Draupadi that she has not only lost her father and brothers but also all her sons. He then asks Nakula to bring Draupadi to him together with all her maternal relations. In the meantime, Nakula, having broken the dreadful news to her, brings her to the battlefield strewn with the mangled bodies of the dead. Trembling with horror and grief she falls in front of Yudhishthira. Bhima steps forward and picks her up in his arms. She does not even have the satisfaction of knowing that her sons were killed in glory on the battlefield fighting bravely for her cause. Grieving and lamenting, but never one to give up, she demands that Ashwatthama be punished for his action. She wants Ashwatthama killed and the gem that he wears on his forehead to be brought to her. She will place that gem on Yudhishthira's crown, she claims, otherwise she will kill herself. She appeals to Bhima to do this deed as he is the strongest and most trustworthy being the only one who has protected her repeatedly. Unable to bear her grief, Bhima leaves to accomplish what she has demanded.

However, this is a dangerous mission and Sri Krishna asks Yudhishthira to take steps for Bhima's protection. Ashwatthama possesses a powerful weapon capable of untold destruction, *Brahmasira*, that his father Dronacharya had given to him. Arjuna, too, as the favourite pupil of Drona, has a similar weapon. However, aware of his son's restlessness Drona had warned him never to use it in battle even when overtaken by the greatest danger and particularly never to use it against human beings. Knowing Ashwatthama, Sri Krishna is sure that he will now use the weapon. He, therefore, mounts his chariot and together with Arjuna and Yudhishthira catches up with Bhima but fails to stop him as he proceeds towards the banks of the River Ganga. Sri Krishna sees Sage Vyasa sitting at the edge of the water surrounded by many rishis and Ashwatthama sitting beside them. Bhima rushes towards him taking up his bow and arrow. Ashwatthama sees Bhima and becomes very agitated. He uses the forbidden *Brahmastra* to defend himself. Sri Krishna orders Arjuna to counter it with his weapon. Veda Vyasa stops the weapons with his powers and thus prevents complete annihilation. He commands that the two retrieve their weapons immediately. Arjuna can withdraw his weapon as directed, but Ashwatthama is unable to do so. Instead, he now directs it to Abhimanyu's progeny in Uttara's womb to destroy any future race as that would mean the end of Pandu's lineage after the passing away of the Pandava brothers. The Kauravas have already been destroyed. The victory is truly an illusory one as the entire Kuru line is threatened with extinction. To prevent this, Sri Krishna promises that he will ensure the birth of Parikshit, Uttara's unborn son and curses Ashwatthama.

Ashwatthama is forced to give Yudhishthira his gem in exchange of which Yudhishthira grants him his life. The Pandavas together with Sri Krishna quickly return to Draupadi and Bhima gives her the gem. He assures her that

Ashwatthama has been truly vanquished in every way but has not been killed out of respect for their deceased preceptor. Bhima reminds her of her bitter words to Sri Krishna when he had made the last attempt at peace. She had reproved him by saying that in effect that she had no sons or husbands and that even Sri Krishna was not her friend since he supported King Yudhishthira's desire for peace. War, says Bhima, has its own dire consequences and she has to accept them. She cannot now break down over the death of her sons. Draupadi says that what she really wanted was that the injury done to them by the Kauravas should be avenged and asks Yudhishthira to wear Ashwatthama's gem on his crown, which he does.

The Pandavas rule for thirty years at the end of which Sri Krishna passes away and the Vrishni race too is destroyed. When Arjuna's Gandiva also becomes powerless, they know that the time has come for them to depart. Handing over the reins of the kingdom to Parikshit, their grandson, they prepare for the final journey of their life to the Himalaya. At the head is Yudhishthira with his brothers following behind — Bhima, Arjuna, Nakula, and Sahdeva. At the end is Draupadi. However, she is the first to fall. As they move on leaving her dying there, Bhima cannot help but ask that why has she, who is so virtuous, fallen first. No one stops to stay by her side. The woman with five husbands dies truly an orphan.

What is her fault all along? She saves her husbands, endures hardships with them, inspires them to fight for their rights and guides them to the throne. Perhaps her fault is that she never surrenders her independence and tries to make the journey of her life as an equal.

5

THE WARRIOR QUEENS

The prize in the *Mahabharata* is the throne of Hastinapura for which the women strive ceaselessly and more relentlessly and determinedly than even the men who are to occupy it. Marriage, sexuality, and politics are all interlinked. Matrimonial alliances are made by men, particularly by Arjuna, on behalf of the Pandavas to consolidate or expand their power base. But the women use their sexuality to grasp *de facto* power, and the husbands and sons are only the means to that end. While patriarchal values may be normative in the *Mahabharata*, powerful matriarchal alternatives are provided by regional romantic alliances between Arjuna and the brave and beautiful warrior queens, proud rulers of independent kingdoms, who are more than a match for him and whom he cannot really subjugate, try as he might. But that is what adds a dash of danger and challenge, making the liaisons even more exciting.

That marriage and politics are interlinked is obvious in the several of Arjuna's marriages in the post-Draupadi phase. Even earlier, Kunti encourages Bhima to marry Hidimbi, the sister of the demon ruler. When he says that he will stay with her only till the birth of a son, she was more than agreeable as she does not want to bind him. Kunti gives her consent to this proposal because she sees in it a way of forging an inalienable political alliance with the forest dwellers. Its usefulness becomes evident in the valour with which Ghatotkacha, Bhima's son from Hidimbi, fights in the *Mahabharata* war, eventually dying a heroic death in his father's cause.

But the primary alliance maker is Arjuna as he travels far and wide after his self-imposed exile according to the rules established between the brothers regarding the sharing of Draupadi. One can argue that it is Arjuna's wounded psyche that prompts him to marry several charismatic women. If he could not have Draupadi to himself, there were other beautiful and independent women, brave warriors ruling their kingdoms with great aplomb who are all ready to unite with him. However, in terms of political significance, it is also a useful way of bringing all these kingdoms into the fold of Hastinapura.

As the *Mahabharata* story spread to the various regions of the country, it collected within it, local myths and traditions through oral narratives and folk performances, many of which incorporate matriarchal values and norms. Arjuna is chosen to wed all these overwhelmingly attractive women because he is the quintessential hero. He is Pandu's son got with a great effort of austerities and divine will. He is exceptional, favoured by the gods and by his teachers, the mainstay of the Pandavas, who performs outstanding feats. He gets celestial weapons, wins the most dynamic and desirable of women as his wives, is the pivot of the *Mahabharata* war, safeguards the kingdom after the performance of the horse sacrifice and it is finally his lineage, his grandson through Abhimanyu, which succeeds to the throne of Hastinapura, carrying on the Kuru dynasty.

He is also the complete individual being, a man but with a thorough knowledge of women as Brihannala. The most handsome of all the Pandavas, it is no wonder that he aligns with beautiful, brave and wise women, individuals in their own right. There is a popular saying in Tamil that one can even count the stars in the sky but not the wives of Arjuna. In the process, some of these stories remain outside the mainstream of the *Mahabharata* while others get integrated after transformation. Those that remain outside may not be very well known but within their own region, they have powerful acceptance and enrich the tapestry of the *Mahabharata*.

One such story pertains to Ulupi, the Naga princess. In his wanderings, Arjuna arrives at the source of the Ganga where he meets Ulupi. While living there with the brahmins, one day he goes as usual into the Ganga to bathe. Just as he is about to come out to perform his daily sacrificial rites before the fire, he is dragged to the bottom of the water by Ulupi who is completely overcome by her attraction to him. She does not reveal herself at the time but carries him away to the beautiful mansion of the king of Nagas. A sacrificial fire has already been lit there for Arjuna and he fearlessly performs his daily rites with great devotion. After he finishes, Ulupi appears, introduces herself to him as the daughter of the Naga king Kauravya, in the line of Airvata. She tells him that she has been overwhelmed with desire since she saw him bathing in the River Ganga. She is still unmarried, she declares, and asks Arjuna to give himself to her that day.

Arjuna is in a quandary. He explains that, as commanded by King Yudhishthira, he is supposed to remain a celibate for twelve years and so is not at liberty to act in any way he likes. He says he is still willing to serve at her pleasure if he can and asks her how that can be done without breaching his vow. Arjuna is obviously tempted. Ulupi answers that she already knows why Arjuna is wandering about in exile and why he has decided on celibacy but she gives an endearingly delicious hair-splitting argument to enable him to circumvent his vow, which the handsome warrior is only too willing to accept. She says that his vow only pertains to Draupadi and not to everyone else. Besides it is his duty to give succour to the distressed and so his virtue will not diminish if he gives her relief in her passion for him. And even if it does, he will gain merit by his saving her life because if he does not accede to her wishes she will destroy herself. As Ulupi pleads and woos Arjuna, he does everything she desires, spending the night in restless delight. Accompanied by Ulupi, he returns the next day, from the palace of Kauravya, to where the River Ganga enters the plains. She then takes leave of him and goes back to her own abode. But before going she grants Arjuna a boon, making him invincible in water saying that he will be victorious over every amphibious creature. Ulupi has a son Iravat by Arjuna whom she raises herself while continuing to remain in her kingdom.

Arjuna meets Chitrangada as he enters the kingdom of Manalur. There is an interesting transformation of the local legend as it is absorbed into the patriarchal mainstream of the *Mahabharata*. Chitrangada is popularly accepted as a Manipuri princess, but she could also have belonged to Tripura. Another possibility put forward is that Manalur could have been in south India from where the tale may have travelled east as the suffix 'ur' is usually given to a non-brahmin settlement in south India.

The legend indicates that Chitrangada is a tribal chieftain or queen whom Arjuna faces in battle, not knowing that he is fighting a woman and is defeated by her. She then falls in love with Arjuna who is totally repulsed by her ugliness. In other words, he cannot come to terms with her 'masculine' qualities as a warrior. To win his love, Chitrangada prays to Shiva and Kamadeva, the God of Love to make her beautiful. Arjuna now marries her but leaves after the birth of a son, Babhruvahana.

In the *Mahabharata*, traces of the matriarchal local legend remain as it is integrated into its patriarchal structure. Arjuna enters the Kingdom of Manipur ruled by king Chitravahana who has a beautiful daughter, Chitrangada. Seeing her he falls in love with her and places a marriage proposal before her father. The latter tells Arjuna of his ancestor, king Prabhanjana, who was childless and who underwent severe ascetic penances to obtain a child. Lord Shiva was pleased and granted him the boon that not only he, but each successive descendant of his race would have only one child. Since then, only one child has been born to every successive generation but all of them have a son each. Chitravahana, however, now only has a daughter whom he looks upon as a son. Therefore, it is she, he says, who will have to carry on his family and hence cannot accompany Arjuna. Only on this condition he is willing to give away his daughter to him. Arjuna agrees to the condition and with Chitrangada as his wife, he lives in the city for three years. When a son is born to Chitrangada, Arjuna embraces her and taking leave of his father-in-law, sets off on his wanderings again, assuring her that she will one day come to Hastinapura and meet Kunti, Draupadi, and the others.

Legend brings Ulupi and Chitrangada together after the Kurukshetra war. When Yudhishthira finally ascend the throne of Hastinapura and performs the Ashwamedha Yagna, Arjuna goes with the army behind the sacrificial horse. It takes him, among other places, once again to Manipur where his son Babhruvahana, accompanied by Brahmins goes out to receive him, carrying precious gifts. However, remembering the duties of a Kshatriya, Arjuna does not approve of it. He wants his son to fight him as he has not come as his father but as the protector of Yudhishthira's sacrificial horse.

When Ulupi hears of Arjuna's harsh words to Babhruva-hana, she is unable to tolerate it. Piercing through the earth, she come to the spot where she sees Babhruvahana looking very upset and urges him to fight his father. Inspired by her, he puts on his armour, gets into his chariot and challenges Arjuna to battle. The fight between father and son is heroic as Babhruvahana pierces Arjuna with his arrows. Babhruvahana's appetite is whetted and Arjuna is delighted with his son's powers. Eventually, Babhruvahana's arrows pierce his fathers' breast; Arjuna falls in a swoon to the earth, slain and defeated. Babhruvahana also faints, both from the fatigue of the battle and from the sorrow of having slain his father.

Hearing that her husband has been killed and that her son is also lying wounded on the ground, Chitrangada comes, greatly agitated and berates Ulupi for the death of their common husband Arjuna. As she laments, Babhruvahana regains consciousness and grieves for the death of his father as he feels guilty of patricide. Both mother and son prepare to starve to death in their sorrow.

Ulupi then brings the gem possessed by the nagas that can bring the dead back to life and revives Arjuna with it. She says that she herself created an illusion as Arjuna is incapable of being defeated by anyone. She just wanted to test his son's skills and valour and that is why she urged Babhruvahana to fight. She assures Babhruvahana that he has not committed any sin by accepting Arjuna's challenge and carrying it through.

Arjuna gets up as if from a dream and asks Babhruvahana why Chitrangada and Ulupi are on the battlefield. Ulupi explains that she has done all this for Arjuna's good. He had slain Bhishma, the son of Shantanu, unrighteously in the battle of Kurukshetra. She merely wants him to be absolved of his sin. Because Arjuna did not defeat Bhishma in a fair fight, having used the stratagem of Sikhandin, he is destined to go to hell. Supported by Ganga, he has been cursed by the Vasus. Having found this out, Ulupi is very disturbed. She penetrates the nether regions and informs her father who, in an anxious and aggrieved state, goes to the Vasus and pleads with them. They tell him that Arjuna has a great son, Babhruvahana, the ruler of Manipur. If Babhruvahana defeats Arjuna on the battlefield and throws him down on the earth, then Arjuna will be freed from the curse. Having found this out, the king of Nagas comes back and informs his daughter Ulupi. She thus plans everything to free Arjuna from the curse.

Further integration into the mainstream and patriarchal norms of the text happens as Ulupi and Chitrangada are shown accompanying Kunti to the forest when she decides to leave Hastinapura for good, together with Gandhari and Dhritarashtra. They later visit them there and wait on them as do the Pandavas.

Rabindranath Tagore, in his musical *Chitra* further transforms the legend. In his retelling, Chitrangada is reared as a son by the king and queen of Manipur. She rules the kingdom and is out hunting in the forest when she meets Arjuna and falls in love with him. She approaches him dressed as a woman, but he refuses her on grounds of his vow of celibacy. She now prays to the God of Love and Beauty so that Arjuna will be irresistibly attracted towards her. This is exactly what happens and Arjuna, compelled by her beauty, breaks his vow.

Chitrangada's rival is now her own body. Her victory over Arjuna is a hollow one as it is built on a falsehood. She is not actually the beautifully seductive woman that he imagines her to be, and she cannot bear to think that he has belittled himself for her by breaking his vow. In desperation, she prays to Madana, the God of Love to restore her original form. Arjuna, too, begins to tire of his love for her when he encounters villagers who are getting ready to fight off marauders. They tell him about their brave warrior queen who protects them like a tigress and loves them like a mother. Arjuna longs to meet her, his equal. Chitrangada in her original form enters her court and demands the right and power to be an equal to Arjuna both in prosperity and in adversity if he still wants to marry her. Arjuna agrees and there is a celebration.

Another important and powerful matrimonial alliance that

Arjuna makes is with Subhadra, Sri Krishna and Balarama's sister. After leaving Chitrangada, Arjuna goes to meet his friend and cousin, Sri Krishna. Here he sees Subhadra and falls in love with her. In another version Balarama wants Subhadra to marry Duryodhana, an alliance that is unacceptable to Sri Krishna. Hence, Sri Krishna happily aids Arjuna to abduct Subhadra and further helps to pacify everyone, including Balarama, who are outraged by Arjuna's actions as they, among other things, consider it to be a breach of their hospitality. When there is a great uproar over Arjuna's action, Sri Krishna restores peace by asserting that Arjuna is a very suitable groom for Subhadra and that it is a matter of honour for their families to be united and for Subhadra to be Arjuna's wife. Thus, the friendship and alliance between them is further cemented. Draupadi, however, gets very jealous when Arjuna returns to Khandavaprastha with Subhadra; she is angry with him. Arjuna begs her forgiveness. Kunti welcomes Subhadra and finally Draupadi accepts her. Subhadra and Arjuna's son, Abhimanyu, plays a significant role in the *Mahabharata* war. Sri Krishna's facilitating Arjuna to marry Subhadra is driven by his knowledge of the role that Abhimanyu has to play and the fact that it is Abhimanyu's son, Parikshit who is the patriarch keeping the lineage alive.

As per indigenous traditions, especially from south India, Arjuna is shown to marry several autonomous warrior queens fearlessly ruling over their realms, like Alli, Pavazhakoddi, and Monnliyal. Apart from sexual conquests, these are also means of making political alliances with various southern kingdoms and of bringing them into the Pandava fold. Here again, can be seen the mingling of patriarchal norms with the matriarchal order. In the ballad of Alli or Alli Kadai, Alli is the only child of a Pandyana king born of immaculate conception as she is found on a lily or an 'alli' flower at the conclusion of a "Putra kameshti Yaga" or a yagna performed to get a son. She is raised as a son and becomes proficient in riding and the martial arts. She defeats Neenmugan, her half-brother, in a fierce battle and is crowned the ruler of the Pandyan Kingdom. Neenmugan himself is said to have had an unusual birth, by the blessings of Shiva and Parvati, being born to a female crow that was transformed into a maiden, and the Pandyan king whose daughter was Alli. Neenmugan is the legitimate heir to the throne as he is crowned king by the royal couple, his parents, before they retire to the forests for a life of meditation and contemplation. Apparently, at this point Alli is not considered suitable for the position of a ruler but Alli considers Neenmugan as a usurper. By defeating Neenmugan she is reputed to have brought glory to Madurai as Neenmugan is a tyrant and incompetent. Whatever may be the case, it is clearly a power struggle between the two in which Alli vanquishes the legitimate heir. Alli herself is a strict ruler who is held in fear and awe by the entire populace.

At this time, the much-married Pandava prince Arjuna, sets out on a long pilgrimage with Sri Krishna during which both enter Madurai in the garb of ascetics. Even today a popular saying in Tamil is "Arjuna Sanyasi", which implies a deceitful hypocrite. Here an innkeeper, according to one version, and a merchant, according to another, recounts to them the valour and beauty of Alli. He tells them of Alli's victory over Neenmugan and her strict rule in Madurai. Arjuna's sarcastic response is that she seems to be a man in female attire, entirely devoid of femininity. This reflects Arjuna's encounter with the warrior queen Chitrangada in which too he finds it difficult to reconcile to her as a warrior or to her 'masculine' qualities.

However, Alli, unlike Chitrangada, who had to pray to the God of love to obtain beauty, is already a stunning woman, a great beauty who excites Arjuna's conquering instincts. She is a challenge to his male ego when he learns that she is a man hater to the extent that all the officials in her government, including the military commanders are women. Even today among Tamilians an all-female household is sarcastically referred to as "Alli Rajyam" or "the administration run by Alli". Once aroused, Arjuna is determined to possess her. It is more a battle of sexes than love and there are issues of power and control between them, which can be read as a clash between the patriarchal and matriarchal norms. Arjuna tries to seduce her in various ways and finally succeeds in marrying her. He enters her bedroom in the shape of a snake given as a gift to her by the disguised Sri Krishna. In her innocence she plays with the snake, which eventually hypnotizes and seduces her. The sexual imagery of the phallic snake is obvious and powerful. There is a graphic description in the ballad of Alli that says that she is exhausted by Arjuna's love play, is drained of all resistance and left drugged with passion. Thus, Arjuna actually cheats and ravishes Alli through deception without her knowledge or consent. She loses her virginity and with that her power.

Before achieving success, he makes several other attempts. In a farcical scene, Arjuna becomes a transvestite, taking the name of Chengamalam and fools Alli into believing that she has a female companion. He goes hunting with her retinue and ensures that she gets caught alone with him. He massages her tired body, and his disguise is so effective that she does not discover his real sex despite the curious emotions that are aroused in her by his touch. Arjuna, after all, enjoys a reputation as an expert at crossdressing. He did spend a year as Brihannala, the eunuch, in the court of Virata teaching dance to Princess Uttara and her companions. In the Alli ballad, while pressing Alli's feet, he gently takes away her ring without her knowledge. It is only when he begins to narrate to her the story of the Pandava princes and the many virtues of Arjuna that Alli suddenly discovers that he is a man and that she has been fooled into spending several intimate hours in his company.

Arjuna manages to escape from the furious and humiliated Alli.

The ballad, *Alli Arasani Malai* by Pugazhendi Pulavar of the sixteenth century, deals with the gradual taming of Alli to fit the patriarchal role model of an ideal wife. Arjuna achieves the ultimate triumph over Alli when he secretly ties the Tali, the yellow thread symbolizing a woman's marital status in the south Indian tradition, around her neck and she conceives the very same night. Alli is full of wrath but her women companions counsel patience as they emphasize upon her that she is now a married woman and a would-be mother. She has, therefore, no option but to reconcile with Arjuna.

The story of Alli after her marriage to Arjuna is continued in three related ballads – *Pavazhakkodi Malai*, *Pulandaran Kalavu Malai*, and *Eni Etram*. Pavazhakkodi is another princess who becomes a victim of Arjuna's desire. It so happens that once Alli's son by Arjuna, Pulandaran, is crying for a toy chariot made of coral. The queen cannot fulfil his wish and so Arjuna sets out in search of it. He comes upon the princess Pavazhakkodi, which literally means the coral creeper, in Themboor. Arjuna, who had seduced Alli as a snake, now ravishes Pavazhakkodi as a swan. In another tale, Arjuna has a wife called Minnoliyal who refuses to live with him because she dislikes him. However, Draupadi invites all his wives for a feast at which she and Alli persuade Minnoliyal to treat Arjuna as a husband.

The next ballad in the Alli Trilogy is *Pulandaran Kalavu Malai*. It deals with Pulandaran who is supposed to marry Duryodhana's daughter or Duryodhana's sister. However, the match is unacceptable to the Kauravas because of family tensions and rivalries. The Alli myth is again central to the ballad of *Eni Etram* in which Duryodhana falls in love with the princess Subhadra, who later becomes one of the chief wives of Arjuna. Alli is furious that Duryodhana should even dare to desire Subhadra whom Arjuna loves. She persuades the love-struck Duryodhana to dance and sing and he is thus mocked and humiliated by Alli.

A significant aspect of the independent queens who marry Arjuna is that each one of them is a political ally as well. However, the myths transform these brave queens into submissive wives to keep Arjuna's territorial authority and dominance intact. Every instance of Arjuna's sexual triumph also constitutes a political victory and the assimilation of one more independent kingdom into the Pandava Empire. Hierarchical structures come into play in these alliances in the public and in the private domain, which makes it necessary to subjugate Alli both politically and personally and make her adhere to the patriarchal norms. Alli is made to reconcile to Arjuna as her husband after he has ravished her, and she has conceived. From a man-hating independent warrior queen she is made so subservient that she goes to any length to make Arjuna happy including procuring wives for him as in the case of Subhadra and of joining hands with Draupadi to persuade Monnliyal to surrender to him as her husband. These actions are totally out of character for both Alli and Draupadi and are only an effort to keep the power structures intact in the private and public domains.

AFTERWORD

The institution of war, politics, kingship, caste, and class are in the public domain and questioning them can only lead to a realigning of outer power structures. But marriage is in the private domain with potential for radical repercussions in the public sphere. If the power structures within the institution of marriage and its accompanying norms are questioned, there is apprehension of sexual anarchy, and the independence of women must be suppressed by men because it threatens their predominance in domestic life. Marriage and family are the backbone of a stable society and of the state. Any disturbance in the marital equation of power disturbs the status quo of the family and the economy of social values. This also accounts for the reluctance of men to allow women to occupy public spaces in a way that can rock the existing hierarchical power structures in private spaces and vice versa. However, despite best efforts, many of these stories often remain outside the patriarchal mainstream of the *Mahabharata* although they are locally powerful. The intermingling of patriarchal norms and matriarchal values is at best, uneasy.

The words of the *Mahabharata* when seen from the point of

view of women is essentially one of power structures, both in the private and public spheres, mainly controlled by men. The women can attain a voice in this world by acting through their status as wives and mothers through their husbands and sons. Their voices, however, are not uni-dimensional. They are characterized by multiple, often conflicting, and ambiguous discourses struggling to articulate themselves. Not a single queen's voice is, therefore, examinable as a resolved one. There is something about every queen that lingers on after every evaluation has been wrapped up, after every perspective has been mapped. This abundant and indefinite presence of the queens is the most striking feature of the *Mahabharata*. The epic's patriarchal world fails to hem them in, although there are other women, unwilling to occupy the uncertain and insecure spaces of these queens. These independent women are perceived as unchaste. Alternatively, they are placed outside the norms by the society that brands them as demons, *apsara*s, or ascetics in a category of 'others', because their unbridled sexuality can so easily destroy this carefully constructed power structure. As wives and mothers, the sexuality of women is subjugated and regulated to fulfilling the societal demands of producing as many sons as possible. However, the women do manage to a create space for themselves within these limitations and become powerful figures capable of changing the course of events. Hence, they become a force to be reckoned with through their own intelligence, acumen, and endeavour. It is more often the men rather than the women who appear indecisive at crucial moments, lacking in sagacity and in need of support to propel them into action.

SELECT READINGS

Abhisheki, Janaki. 1998. *Tales and Teaching of the Mahabharata.* Mumbai: Bharatiya Bhavan.

Bhattacharyya, Sudhisankar. 1971. *Imagery in the Mahabharata: Influence on Later Sanskrit Literature.* Calcutta: Pustak Bhandar.

Carriere, Jean-Claude. 2001. Trs. Aruna Vasudev. *In Search of the Mahabharata: Notes of Travels in India with Peter Brooks.* Delhi: Macmillan India Ltd.

Deshphande, C.R. 1978. *Transmission of the Mahabharata Tradition.* Shimla: Indian Institute of Advanced Study.

Frasca, Richard, A. 1998. *Pancali Capatam* (The Vow of Draupadi). Images of Ritual and Political Liberation in Tamil Theatre. *The Drama Review*. Vol. 38, No. 38, No. 2, pp. 89-103.

Ganguli, Kisari Mohan. 1970. Trans. *The Mahabharata*, 12 Vols. Delhi: Munshiram Manoharlal.

Haddon, A.C. 1902. Fire-walking in Southern India. *Folklore.* Vol. 13, No. 1, pp. 89.90.

Hill, Peter. 2001. *Fate, Predestination and Human Action in the Mahabharata: A Study in the History of Ideas.* Delhi: Munishiram Manoharlal Publishers Pvt. Ltd.

Hiltebeitel, Alf. 1976. *The Ritual of Battle: Krishna in the Mahabharata.* Ithaca and London: Cornell University Press.

Hiltebeitel, Alf. 1999. *Draupadi among Rajputs, Muslims and Dalits: Rethinking India's Oral and Classical Epics.* Delhi: Oxford University Press.

Jhanji, Rekha. 1995. *Human Condition in the Mahabharata.* Shimla: Indian Institute of Advanced Study.

Johnson, Elizabeth A. 1996. Does God Play Dice? Divine Providence and Chance. *Theological Studies.* Vol. 56 (1996), pp. 3-18.

Karmarkar, A.P. 1962. Religion and Philosophy of the Epic. *The Cultural Heritage of India.* Vol. II. Calcutta: The Ramakrishna Mission Institute of Culture.

Karve, Irawati. 1994. *Yuganta: The End of an Epoch.* Bangalore, Bhopal, Delhi: Orient Longman Ltd.

Lal P. 1980. Trs. *The Mahabharata of Vyasa.* Delhi: Vikas.

Mahendale, M.A. 1995. *Reflections on the Mahabharata War.* Shimla: Indian Institute of Advanced Study.

Matilal, Bimal Krishna, ed. 1989. *Moral Dilemmas in the Mahabharata.* Shimla, Delhi: Indian Institute of Advanced Study in association with Motilal Banarsidass.

Mishra, Vidyaniwas. 1981. *Mahabharata Ka Satya, Parampara Bandhan Nahin.* Delhi: Rajpal and Sons.

Mishra, Vidyaniwas. 1981. *Bhartiya Itihasvidh Aur Bharata Ka Prabuddh Manas, Parampara Bandhan Nahin.* Delhi: Rajpal and Sons.

Mishra, Vidyaniwas. 1985. *Mahabharata Ka Kavyartha.* Delhi, Allahabad: National Publishing House.

Ramaswami, Vijaya. 2002. *The Taming of Alli.* Altantis. Vol. 27.1, Fall/Winter. pp 71-80.

Raychaudhiuri, Hemchandra. 1962. The *Mahabharata*: Some Aspects of its Culture. *The Cultural Heritage of India* Vol. II. Calcutta: The Ramakrishna Mission Institute of Culture.

Sax, William S. ed. 1955. *The Gods at Play*. New York, Oxford: Oxford University Press.

Sharma, Kavita A. 2021. Trs. *Mahabharat ki Maharaniyan*. New Delhi: Sasta Sahitya Mandal Prakashan.

Sharma, Kavita A. and Indu Ramchandani. 2018. *Life Is As Is: Teachings of the Mahabharata*. New Delhi: Wisdom Tree.

Singh, K.S. ed. 1993. *The Mahabharata in the Tribal and Folk Traditions of India*. Shimla: Indian Institute of Advance Study.

Sri Aurobindo. May 1989. *Greatness of the Ramayana and the Mahabharata. A Compilation*. Pondicherry: Sri Aurobindo Society.

Suktankar, V.S. 1957. *The Meaning of the Mahabharata*. Bombay: The Asiatic Society of Bombay.

Sullivan, M. Bruce. 1999. *Seer of the Fifth Veda: Krsna Dvaipayana Vyasa*. Delhi: Motilal Banarsidass Publishers Pvt. Ltd.

Sutherland, Sally J. 1984. Sita and Draupadi: Aggressive Behaviour of the Female Role-Models in the Sanskrit Epics. *Journal of the American Oriental Society*. Vol. 109, No: 1, pp. 63-79.

Sutton, Nicholas. 2000. *Religious Doctrines in the Mahabharata*. Delhi: Motilal Banarsidass Publishers Pvt. Ltd.

Thadani, N.V. 1935. *The Mystery of the Mahabharata*. 5 Vols. Karachi: Bharat Publishing House.

Vaidya, P.L. and A.D. Pusalker. 1939. 1st edition, enlarged 1962. "The Mahabharata: Its History and Character". *The Cultural Heritage of India*. Vol. III. Calcutta: The Ramakrishna Mission, Institute of Culture.